Merv Griffin's
Crosswords
Pocket
Volume 1

100 Very Easy
Crossword Puzzles

Edited by
Timothy Parker

St. Martin's Paperbacks

MERV GRIFFIN'S CROSSWORDS POCKET VOLUME I

Copyright © 2007 by Merv Griffin Enterprises.
Cover photo of Merv Griffin © Merv Griffin Entertainment. Cover photo of Ty Treadway © Aaron Rapoport.

ISBN: 0-312-94689-9
EAN: 978-0-312-94689-0

Printed in the United States of America

St. Martin's Paperbacks edition / October 2007

St. Martin's Paperbacks are published by St. Martin's Press, 175 Fifth Avenue, New York, NY 10010.

10 9 8 7 6 5 4 3 2 1

Merv Griffin's

Crosswords
Pocket
Volume 1

DARE TO COMPARE

ACROSS

1 Distinctive clothing
5 Kiddie-lit trio
10 Memorial column, briefly
14 "Diamonds ___ Girl's Best Friend"
15 Seagirt bit of land
16 Howard and Silver
17 Extremely vain
20 "Twelve Days of Christmas" group
21 Purpose of The Betty Ford Center
22 "God bless us ___ one"
23 Plato's marketplace
25 Trackside offer
28 Type of mother
29 Pentagon personnel
30 Distinctive atmosphere
31 Silas Marner, early on
33 Citified
34 Nearly powerless
38 Hot trend
39 Bill in Washington?
40 Where you are?
41 They hold the line
43 Kind of service
46 "Howard's ___" (1992 Oscar winner)
47 On tenterhooks
48 Notions
50 Respond to stimuli
52 Sumatran apes
53 Bullheaded
57 Humorous Bombeck
58 They hold their horses
59 They're found in pockets
60 "___ does it"
61 "Animal House" house
62 New Jersey squad

DOWN

1 Like Lauren Hutton's front teeth
2 Achieve stardom
3 Begin again, as a debate
4 Eddie, founder of a retail company
5 Unreasonable inclination
6 Superman's logo
7 What's put before the carte?
8 Some print jobs, briefly
9 Mans the helm
10 Deep sea threat
11 Television, slangily
12 "Murder, ___" (1960 film)
13 Discouraging sound
18 Butterless, as toast
19 Sound of insight
23 Mars' counterpart
24 Repair shops
26 Armenia neighbor
27 No-star review, e.g.
29 Tenderfoot's org.
30 Sciences' partner
31 Perplexing path, especially to a rat

Puzzle 1 by Fran & Lou Sabin

32 1952 and 1956 campaign name
33 SUV's cousin
34 Common songbird
35 Hearing aids
36 Curly-leafed vegetable
37 "___ My Party" (Lesley Gore hit)
38 "The Motorcycle Diaries" subject
41 Save for later viewing
42 Course for a gourmand
43 Academic achievement
44 Bald baby bird
45 Pass judgment on
47 Computer key
48 "Rosemary's Baby" author Levin
49 "Good Will Hunting" star
51 Auctioneerless auction site
52 Thessalian mount
53 Neither fold nor raise
54 Singsong sound
55 Soccer's zero
56 Doodlebug's prey

COLOR MY WORLD

ACROSS

1 "Love Boat" character
6 Bombay wraparound dress
10 Improvisational music style
14 "Purlie" star Moore
15 Dr. Seuss' "If ___ the Circus"
16 Type of slinger
17 Inflate, as with pride
18 Not tacit
19 He's no pro
20 Seldom
23 Legendary baseball star Ripken
24 Takes the wheel
25 Tempest setting
29 They're drawn to the flame
31 Perry's penman
32 Clark or Gibbs of country music
33 "The Murders in the Rue Morgue" beast
36 Hercule Poirot's pride
40 Sheep's milieu
41 Films with casts of thousands
42 Partner of "read 'em"
43 More than lionize
44 Sixth Amendment adjective
46 Film mouse
49 Golf norm
50 Gives up
57 Jack-in-the-pulpit, for one
58 Grimace inducer
59 Replay effect
60 Sport of princes
61 Excalibur's handle
62 All agog
63 First name in slapstick
64 D-Day invasion town
65 Steakhouse selection

DOWN

1 "___ Excited" (Pointer Sisters hit)
2 No longer bursting at the seams?
3 Baldwin of "30 Rock"
4 Having the right stuff
5 Colorful cat
6 Strong cordage fiber
7 Damascus resident
8 Snooker cushion
9 Automotive, steel or tourism, e.g.
10 Brings dishonor to
11 Birchbark boat
12 Noted capitalist John Jacob
13 Dilutes
21 First name among legendary crooners
22 Moral philosophy
25 "William ___ Overture"
26 Canal or Lake
27 Ski resort next to Snowbird
28 Astro, Scooby-Doo or Dino, e.g.
29 Benevolence
30 Lode yields
32 Working for the weekend letters

Puzzle 2 by Ron Halverson

33 Away from the sea wind
34 Argued a claim
35 Catch sight of
37 Come-hither looks
38 They're often etched in stone
39 Female with a wool coat
43 Mythological being between gods and humans
44 Remained unused

45 Like some stations on a car radio
46 Pulls a switcheroo
47 Clairvoyant's cards
48 Tongue neighbor
49 Mottled horse
51 Display one's patience
52 It could cause one to switch gears
53 Bodybuilder's bane
54 Recognizable symbol
55 Clifton Davis sitcom
56 "An Inconvenient Truth" star

BLINK TWICE

ACROSS

1 Course taken after trig, often
5 January 2 event
9 Bureau
14 Nabisco cookie
15 Product mention
16 Star-crossed lover
17 "___ me up, Scotty!"
18 Indian tourist mecca
19 Allow inside
20 Star of 38-Across
23 Benz ending
24 Cost to be dealt in
25 Fitted within one another
27 Nova follower
30 Brief contact
32 Tin Man's desire
33 Transmission part
34 Electrifying swimmers?
38 Hit show starring 20-Across
41 Plateau relative
42 London Magazine essayist
43 Born yesterday
44 Not the final copy
46 School notebook
47 Bedtime recitation
50 Interstate hauler
51 Female octopus
52 Co-star of 20-Across
58 Isolated
60 26 of 32 counties of Ireland
61 Highly rated
62 Beauty parlor
63 Where most humans reside
64 Social blunder for Nanette?
65 Put forth effort
66 Fermented honey beverage
67 Laurel in "The Music Box"

DOWN

1 "On the Waterfront" star Lee J.
2 Wilderness or staging, e.g.
3 Shakespearean king
4 Prepared for battle
5 Rival of Athens
6 Pond growth
7 Fly on a hook
8 Yipes!
9 Large waders
10 Mortar tray
11 Irish patriot Robert
12 Parisian waterway
13 Packed a gun
21 Rita in "West Side Story"
22 Get used (to) (Var.)
26 Deceitful tricks
27 Wooden gap-filler
28 Relinquish
29 They row, row, row your boat

Puzzle 3 by Gayle Dean

30 Suit
31 Indian prince
33 It's played in rounds
35 Camelot character
36 Like early television
37 Tarot reader
39 Stiller's partner
40 Opposite of persona
45 Cry uncle
46 Blow the foam off a brew?
47 Distinct stage
48 Hang loose

49 American chameleon
50 It's over Jordan, on a map
53 Twenty quires
54 Ascend
55 Like some points
56 "___ and the King of Siam"
57 Type of big city light
59 Here-there link

PRETTY UGLY

ACROSS

1 "Zebras," in sports slang
5 Western search party
10 Like the ark during the flood
14 Captive race in "The Time Machine"
15 "Goldengirl" star, Susan
16 Role for Hanks
17 Modern type of message
18 Battle souvenirs
19 Military post
20 Guesser's oxymoron
23 Swabbie
24 Paris abductee
25 It's all the craze
28 Wasting food, e.g. (according to Mom)
30 Scoffed at
34 Planet inhabitants of film
36 Shoebox marking
38 "Cheers" character
39 Polltaker's oxymoron
43 The absolute minimum
44 "Erie Canal" mule
45 Calendar abbr.
46 Some foot bones
49 Catch, to Hamlet
51 River of Scotland
52 He voiced "The Lion King's" Scar
54 ___-jongg
56 Undecided's oxymoron

61 Autobahn auto, perhaps
62 Call forth
63 Invisible emanation
65 Pride of one in a pride
66 Find a new tenant for
67 Cereal for kids
68 Unlike Godiva
69 One-way transports
70 Actress Daly

DOWN

1 Soak in water
2 Gen. Robt. ___
3 "Sanford and Son" star Redd
4 Occupy, as a table
5 Napoleon and Danish
6 Formerly
7 Squirrel away
8 Categorized
9 Store fodder
10 Some Kosovo residents
11 Word with "love" or "bucket"
12 Settle (into)
13 Lime drink
21 ___ in Charles
22 Left Bank "Thank you"
25 Rock fracture
26 Sleep disorder
27 Exclude from practice
29 Separator of family names
31 Cut partner
32 Skip the ceremony

Puzzle 4 by Ron Halverson

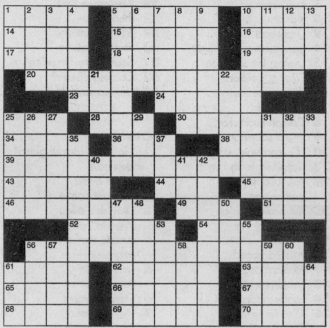

33 "The Divine Comedy" poet
35 Cowardly
37 Both Begleys
40 Video game system name
41 Boathouse item
42 Takes a dive
47 Solitary figures
48 Tearfully complain
50 Ewe said it
53 Broke a commandment
55 Hilton alternative

56 Twofold
57 Novelist Ferber
58 Just got by
59 Suppress, as emotions
60 Ireland, in verse
61 Gremlin's creator
64 Hacker's tool

GROUP DYNAMIC

ACROSS

1 Eye accenter
5 Adroit
9 Unrefined
14 Inauguration highlight
15 Lasting introduction
16 "The ___ Hilton"
17 Recognize the intentions
18 Carson successor
19 ___ a sour note
20 "Celebration" singers
23 Confined (with "up")
24 Palindromist's preposition
25 Big promotion at Fenway
28 Partiality
30 Atlanta-based medical org.
33 Fable monsters
34 Loafer adornment
35 "The Drew Carey Show" setting
36 Front-runner
39 Reverse
40 Stew or miscellany
41 Call again, in poker
42 ___-Foy, Quebec
43 Hit like Ruth
44 "Gunsmoke" star
45 Curative waters
46 Beginning on
47 Unidentifiable one
54 Like some tabloid stories
55 Reason for an "R" rating, perhaps
56 Part of a billiard table
58 Apologize and then some
59 Triumphant cry
60 Strong impulse
61 Source of corruption
62 Chicken dinner?
63 Unpleasant situation

DOWN

1 "To Kill a Mockingbird" character
2 Put in order of significance
3 "A Fish Called Wanda" character
4 Archie Bunker expression
5 Dana of "Fly Away Home"
6 Meet segment
7 ___ off (repel)
8 Race pace
9 Long-running sitcom
10 Singer's asset
11 Wing-prayer link
12 Any time now
13 Turn state's evidence
21 Purchase alternative
22 Tract of wasteland
25 Tough pill to swallow
26 Word with "secret" or "press"
27 Carpentry, acting or plumbing, e.g.
28 Suit
29 Avid about

Puzzle 5 by Mark Milhet

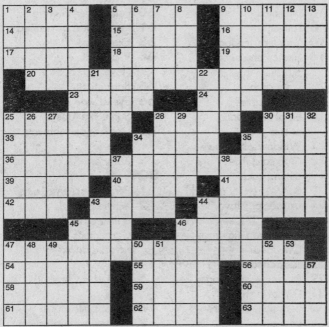

30 "Fletch" star
31 Cubes
32 Popular sodas
34 Burger and fries go-with
35 Type of discussion
37 "Laugh-In" co-host
38 Fielder's flub
43 Web master?
44 Go to a higher level
45 Left Bank river
46 Eagle's nest
47 Pocket cover
48 Jam component?

49 Cacophonous cornfield critter
50 End-of-the-week letters
51 Hockey legend Gordie
52 House antecedent or follower
53 Thinks something is groovy
57 Article written by Rousseau

I'LL DRINK TO THAT!

ACROSS

1 Not exactly, informally
6 Louver
10 Yodeler's feedback
14 Like all crossword puzzles
15 Point at the dinner table?
16 Bit of turbulence, at sea
17 Window alternative
18 "You said it!"
19 Betting odds
20 Bon ___ (witty remark)
21 Carpenter's favorite drink?
24 Himalayan sightings
26 On video
27 Large headline
29 Protective coverings
31 "What a shame"
32 Semiskilled talker?
34 Entice
38 Flowery wreath
39 Clay pigeons, e.g.
41 Delighted exclamation
42 Bar brawl, e.g.
44 Assuage
45 About, contractually
46 It may be cultured
48 Showy bird's mate
50 Helping hand for the Addams family
52 Medicinal plant
53 Entomologist's favorite drink?

56 Company, proverbially
59 Pertaining to planes
60 Folk singer Guthrie
61 Not bottled or canned
63 Exalted poet
64 Word with "love" or "hot"
65 Sabbatical
66 Eyelid woe
67 Some are tops
68 Like a superhighway

DOWN

1 Pyramid scheme, e.g.
2 A little of this, a little of that
3 Carpenter's second favorite drink?
4 ___ Aviv
5 Start of a Christmas carol
6 Great balls of fire
7 Whitewash ingredient
8 From the top
9 Take care of, as a nurse
10 Solar event
11 Onion-flavored garden plant
12 Sharpened to a fine edge
13 Letters with 0
22 About
23 They might send you down the river
25 Nanny's three
27 Aromatic salve

Puzzle 6 by Kendall Twigg

28 Nautical direction
29 Stately
30 Feldspar and others
33 "Song of the South" honorific
35 Woody Allen's favorite drink?
36 Skin
37 "___ He Kissed Me" (1963 Crystals hit)
39 They're coming of age
40 Conical shelter
43 Daily soap dish?
45 Bond's Fleming

47 Struck with consternation
49 Sign up
50 It's hoped for on Halloween
51 Potter of literature
52 Some are blind
53 Chews the fat
54 Black and white goodie
55 Tony candidate
57 Surfer's surface
58 Viewpoints page, briefly
62 PBS funder

IT'S ON ME

ACROSS

1 Two vocal quartets, e.g.
6 Comparative connector
10 Straw in the wind
14 Exaggerated comedy
15 San ___ (Riviera resort)
16 Livingstone sought its source
17 Nonconformist
19 12/26 event
20 "Come ___ About Me" (Supremes)
21 Metrical foot
22 Drew a bead on
23 "___ Action Hero"
25 Substitutes
28 Stains
30 "Picnic" playwright
31 Classic TV's Bee, for one
32 Evangelist McPherson
34 "Dunston Checks In" star
37 Independent journalist
41 Small boy
42 Suburbanite's tool
43 Refrigerated bar
44 Comedic straight man
45 Parts of a corolla
47 Ran at top speed
51 Pizzazz
52 Construction-site sight
53 Truckee stop?
55 Part of an exchange
58 Wander
59 Uncensored opinion
62 Declare
63 "The ___ McCoys"
64 Growing outward
65 Small liqueur glass
66 Probability quote
67 Thick as a brick

DOWN

1 Murders, mob-style
2 "If I Didn't ___" (Ink Spots)
3 Like a picturesque street
4 "Detective" role for Jim Carrey
5 Choose to refrain
6 Svelte
7 Some have medicinal properties
8 "What Kind of Fool ___"
9 Word in most of the Ten Commandments
10 Type of kick
11 ___ Sound Machine
12 First name in talk show hosts
13 Requirements
18 Butter servings
22 Wrath
24 Cost of cards
26 Race official
27 Once more
28 Roosevelt's successor
29 Distinctive quality
32 Secret motive

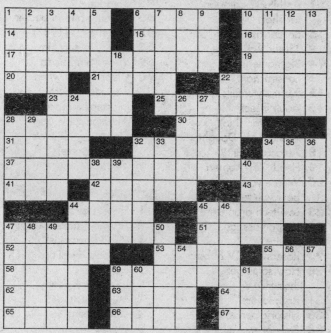

33 Crunchable cubes
34 Having great strength
35 Lime cover
36 Cupid's equivalent
38 Director known for spaghetti Westerns
39 Collier's portal
40 Teensy amount
44 Elaborate attire and accessories
45 Stationer's supply
46 Skipped the big wedding?
47 Take to the dump

48 Mormon settlement
49 Poe's corvine visitor
50 Fear
54 Marine wrigglers
56 It's after John
57 "My country 'tis of ___"
59 Back, once you go "to"
60 Color of a common octagon
61 Cordoba-to-Valencia dir.

CORE VALUES

ACROSS

1 Architect's criterion, for short
5 Border on
9 "Sister Act" attire
14 Big name in construction
15 It usually smells great
16 Adult insect
17 Setting for "Not Without My Daughter"
18 Autocrat: Var.
19 He hit 755 homers
20 Where you might be if you're lost
23 Low-tech propeller
24 Hydromassage facility
25 Roseanne's TV hubby
28 How some get their HDTV
31 Rock layers
36 Historic periods
38 Stew or miscellany
40 Spells
41 Equilibrium point
44 Wing
45 Beguiling trick
46 Tender to the touch
47 Professional's antithesis
49 Words with "record" or "trap"
51 Hulk Hogan once worked on it
52 "Back to the Future" star Thompson
54 It may have a silver lining?
56 Joseph Conrad novella
65 Boredom
66 Causing one to pucker
67 "Blind ___" (1987)
68 1998 DeNiro film
69 View from Toledo
70 Wear gloves when working in here
71 Informal vernacular
72 Audition for a part
73 "Jesus ___" (Bible's shortest verse)

DOWN

1 Pickens of "Hee Haw"
2 "Frasier" actress Gilpin
3 "Good heavens!"
4 Upscale dwelling
5 Frontal
6 Legendary clown
7 Mil. branch
8 Gull cousins
9 Longfellow's Native American hero
10 Asian nursemaid
11 In the buff
12 Grandpa Munster's bat
13 Vocal stress
21 Terhune's "___: a Dog"
22 Photo ___ (media events)
25 Bumper sticker, e.g.
26 Fight card locale
27 Fran Drescher role
29 "___ Dancing" (Johnny Rivers song)
30 Elvis played on them

Puzzle 8 by Matthew J. Koceich

32 Guns the engine
33 Widely accepted saying
34 Brightly colored aquarium fish
35 Thus far
37 Cherry handle
39 Look at with amorous intentions
42 Glorifying
43 Made a verbal comeback
48 "The Matrix" hero
50 Sacred chest

53 "The Morning ___" (Jane Fonda film)
55 Provide with income
56 Bride's towel word
57 Organic compound
58 "___ and the King of Siam"
59 Archaeological site
60 "Where Eagles ___" (1969)
61 Elaborate solo
62 Icicle hangout
63 One of Hitchcock's 39
64 Making its way

WAY TO GO!

ACROSS

1 ___ to riches
5 Kind of life
10 Political competition
14 "The ___ thickens"
15 One-on-one learner
16 Run ___ (go wild)
17 Lemurs' land
19 "The ___ Show" (Chuck Barris)
20 "Independence Day" star
21 Morality tales
23 Readies for surgery
25 First-day-of-class handout
27 Baskin-Robbins purchase
28 Suitable to the occasion
30 Words with "directions" or "likelihood"
31 Taylor hubby before Fisher
32 Perfectly correct
35 Spot for a mud bath?
36 Avid reader's complaint
39 Time division
42 Consecrate
43 Congers, e.g.
47 Paint variety
49 Sound of amazement
50 "K-i-s-s-i-n-g" place
51 Keller's "miracle worker"
54 Watch for
55 Do-gooders' interests
56 Currency west of the Urals
58 "Clear and Present Danger" star
59 Agog over the rich and famous
63 Winter Olympics event
64 Removes extraneous material
65 Homer setting
66 Found a function for
67 Type of panel
68 Didn't draw a card

DOWN

1 33, 45, or 78
2 Menu phrase
3 Unexpected boon
4 Panicky onrush
5 "ER" exclamation
6 "Silence!"
7 Et al. relative
8 Like some vegetables
9 Born to be wild
10 Sleeve type
11 Biology class captives
12 Seek the advice of
13 Heart readout, for short
18 Grunts, so to speak
22 Russian pancakes
23 Fractional amt.
24 Kanga's kid
25 London's Paddington, for one
26 Sylvester Stallone, to fans

Puzzle 9 by Lynn Lempel

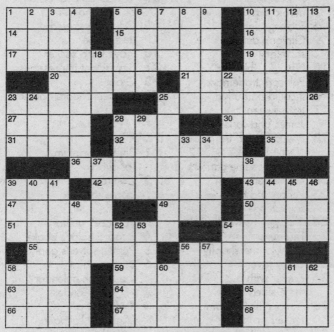

28 Gulf near the Red Sea

29 Cancun coin

33 First James Bond film

34 Hippocratic pronouncement

37 Vertical graph component

38 Bottom-line value

39 Some railways

40 Unpleasantly loud

41 Wanted by the police

44 It may leave a smudge

45 Island memento

46 Part of a musical gig

48 Lost one's tail?

52 Three-piece pieces

53 Roger Clemens, in 2004

54 Serious hang-ups?

56 Columnist Bombeck

57 KGB whereabouts

58 It might give you chills

60 Take to the sickbed

61 Oliver North's rank (Abbr.)

62 "The Spanish Tragedy" dramatist

JUNGLE FEVER

ACROSS

1 Narrative of heroic exploits
5 Table grains
9 Clinton's defense secretary
14 "The ___ thickens"
15 Polecat's trademark
16 It could be stuffed
17 It's between James and Jones
18 It was hotstuff in "Dante's Peak"
19 Y chromosome carriers
20 Convenience item
23 Put an end to something?
24 ". . . ___ I saw Elba"
25 Disfigure
28 Humble and shoofly
31 Curry favor
36 Rapier with a three-sided blade
38 "Free Willy" animal
40 Frasier or Niles
41 African ruler?
44 Resurrected
45 Televangelist Roberts
46 "___ the Robinsons" (2007)
47 City in the Ukraine or Texas
49 Derek of Derek and the Dominos
51 Flat sound?
52 Up to, in ads
54 Feminine subject
56 Gut reactions
65 Shade of pink
66 Allot
67 Song for the fat lady?
68 Words with "directions" or "likelihood"
69 One of a storied threesome
70 Plays for a sucker
71 Significant impressions
72 Globes
73 Clement Moore opener

DOWN

1 Blueprint datum, for short
2 Controversial apple spray
3 "Earth in the Balance" author Al
4 Road scholar's book?
5 Puzzle solver's goal
6 6th month of the Jewish calendar
7 "___ Me Tender"
8 "Without a ___" (Anthony LaPaglia series)
9 Embark on
10 Norwegian ruler
11 Aloha State port
12 "___ After" (Barrymore film)
13 Last word in the title of a Jack Nicholson classic
21 Gregory Hines film or specialty
22 Piece of mine?
25 Paris underground
26 Plant louse
27 Entertainer Della

Puzzle 10 by Ron Halverson

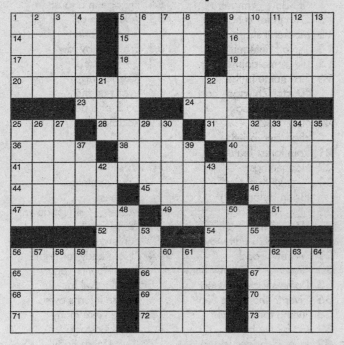

29 Proof word
30 Something to keep
32 Apothecary weight
33 Lightens the load
34 Puts in chips
35 What the defense does, sometimes
37 ___ out (gets by)
39 Place to worship from
42 Loads software
43 Scorches verbally
48 Suffer somewhat
50 "The Sweetheart of Sigma ___"

53 Imaginary place for lost items
55 Make into a statute
56 Kind of test or rain
57 Amount in a Christie title
58 Rafsanjani's home
59 Shake alternative
60 Poetic contraction
61 Shot in the dark
62 Vocalist Sheryl
63 Yothers of "Family Ties"
64 Disrespect verbally

BOOK 'EM!

ACROSS

1 "If I do ___ myself . . ."
6 Chip in for a hand
10 Mackerel shark
14 ___ off (intermittently)
15 Like some points
16 First name in the "Doctor Zhivago" cast
17 Go by the book
20 "L.A. Law" character, briefly
21 Rain forest feature
22 Happenings
23 "___ With a Kiss" (Brian Hyland hit)
25 "___ Paradiso" (1966 film)
27 Anatomical pathway
29 "A Few Good ___"
30 "Peter ___" (Disney film)
33 Dome-shaped dessert
36 River to the Baltic Sea
38 Tuning fork's output
39 Go by the book
42 Inner Hebrides island
43 "Singin' in the Rain" name
44 Shoelace part
45 Spearheaded
46 Rocky hill
47 Broken to the saddle
49 Poker players' ploy
51 Leapt
55 Trees with trembling leaves
58 Throb
60 "A ___ of the Mind," Shepard drama

61 Go by the book
64 Engage in a joust
65 Aftermath of a brainstorm
66 Establish by law
67 "___ & Janis" (comic strip)
68 Word on the back of a penny
69 Recipient

DOWN

1 Couch potatoes' perches
2 Make ___ of (jot down)
3 "Big Three" conference site
4 "Not Ready for Prime Time Players" pgm.
5 You'll travel far before it turns over
6 There were many at Woodstock
7 "___ Dallas Forty"
8 Pool temperature tester
9 Catchall phrase
10 Naomi Campbell, e.g.
11 Line of parishioners?
12 "Critique of Pure Reason" author
13 Table scraps
18 "___ Sargasso Sea" (1993)
19 Disney show "___ Stevens"
24 Tripoli's country
26 Brunch order, perhaps

Puzzle 11 by Gayle Dean

28 "The King of the Cowboys"
30 Combine, as resources
31 "___ of Green Gables"
32 Tree house, of sorts
33 Cookbook instruction
34 Philharmonic instrument
35 Repair
37 Demand payment of
38 Calvin's pal Hobbes
40 Devoted to one's own interests
41 Fiddled (with)

46 It may be full of gas
48 Former Davis Cup coach Arthur
49 Right-hand page
50 Corroded
52 Poe's middle name
53 Bridget Fonda, to Jane
54 "Beau ___"
55 Hammett's terrier
56 "___ Crazy" (Pryor film)
57 Rx unit
59 Gabfest
62 Pindar specialty
63 Crazy eights cousin

GUY TALK

ACROSS

1 Magic Dragon
5 Bean spillers
9 It consists of high spirits
13 Ending with "buck" or "stink"
14 Be a verbal rubber stamp
15 Game surface, sometimes
16 "All in the Family" producer
17 Revered expert
18 Sane
19 TOM
22 Hag
23 Valentine's Day's signature color
24 Pampered
27 Fertility goddess
29 Support system?
32 Last of a series
33 One who looks down a lot?
34 "___ here long?"
35 FRANK
38 Change Money?
39 Dwarf's refrain words
40 Paquin and Pavlova
41 Hole that's inhabitable
42 Something to build on
43 In a warm, comfortable way
44 Antagonist
45 Muffled sounds of impact

47 OSCAR
54 Chocolate source
55 Mound miscue
56 The younger Guthrie
57 Tedium
58 "The Lake ___ of Innisfree"
59 Word processor command
60 Boy Scout's undertaking
61 "What happened next . . ."
62 Cubicle fixture

DOWN

1 Lifeline locale
2 Fertilizer ingredient
3 One with a stable family?
4 Seeing ahead
5 Admiration
6 Sharp or severe
7 CHUCK
8 Like some dough
9 Off one's ___ (crazy)
10 Shortage
11 Canal of song
12 Jacuzzi action
15 Rhythm partner
20 Use a crib sheet
21 "Survivor" group
24 Apt to doodle, perhaps
25 Potassium ___

Puzzle 12 by Mark Milhet

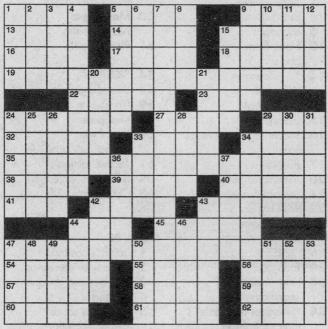

26 "___ the Beguine"
28 Manhattan area
29 Extraterrestrial, e.g.
30 Of the kidneys
31 Tending to fidget
33 Words with "goes" or "seems"
34 Item in some family games
36 Fence supplier
37 Cute zoo bear
42 "Me too" relative
43 Like some treasures

44 Better Business Bureau subject
46 Berry that's easy on the eyes
47 Got a hole in one on
48 Grow faint
49 Troubling marks for high schoolers?
50 Brief note in passing?
51 Item for certain surgeons
52 Automaker Ransom
53 Mobile castle

CLOTHES SHOPPING

ACROSS

1 Accumulated, as a bill
6 Misprint
10 Stone from Down Under
14 "___ Teenage Werewolf" (1957 film)
15 Glean
16 Soccer legend from Brazil
17 JEANS
20 Asner and Sullivan
21 Swabbie's stick
22 Walking on air
23 Sushi choice
24 Dull
25 PANTS
30 Tad's dad
33 New York city near Rome
34 "Sleepless in Seattle" director Ephron
35 Rosebud of filmdom
36 It makes waves
37 Free ride, in a tournament
38 Camp cook's meal
39 Easy clip for Cobalt Blue
40 South-of-the-border order
41 It may be kicked
42 Certain sib
43 SHORTS
45 Plane alternative
46 Scratch (out)

47 Another south-of-the-border order
50 Memphis-to-Nashville dir.
51 Place to put stock in?
54 SKIRT
58 Site of many firings
59 Conductor Klemperer
60 Word with "hand" or "arm"
61 Jacuzzi action
62 Subject or object
63 Out of date

DOWN

1 Bailiff's command
2 Filled with reverence
3 Catches in a dragnet
4 Expend
5 Spaghetti sauce topper, sometimes
6 Word with "bear" or "fly"
7 It's tender to the Japanese
8 Shoe insert
9 "Hamlet" victim
10 Bookish hostess
11 Bombard
12 Spiny plant
13 Beyond off-color
18 Strange sport
19 Pertaining to wings
23 Disney draw
24 Lacking

Puzzle 13 by Lynn Lempel

25 Sailboat propellants
26 Gaming trailblazer
27 Missile shelters
28 Having posted bond
29 British automaking pioneer
30 One might stand up in court
31 Contradict
32 Changes one's story?
35 Barbershop request
38 Gets emotional
40 Checked for size
43 Like many a newborn

44 Diner's card
45 Not fair?
47 Filmmaking unit
48 Fervent
49 Penicillin producer
50 Bus. course
51 Compresses, as a file
52 Upright figures?
53 Shrek, for one
55 Former Japanese Prime Minister Hirobumi
56 Alphabetical nickname
57 Relaxing resort

ALPHABET FOR BEGINNERS

ACROSS

1 "The Simpsons" character Krabappel
5 Kitchen wear
10 Pro ___
14 Capsize (with "over")
15 Gullible
16 "___ the Roof" (Drifters hit)
17 Potential virus carrier
20 Type of acid
21 Sax type
22 Well-known closing trio
23 It may open Windows
25 Not certifiable, so to speak
27 Actor Chaney
30 It's capped and may be slapped
32 Aptly named flight
36 "___ out?" (dealer's query)
38 Remote rooms?
40 Morgan Freeman/Brad Pitt thriller
41 Photographer's concern
44 Metronome speed
45 It gets flat when it's old
46 Get the pot going
47 Braces for impact
49 New Haven school
51 It goes over the road
52 Gin flavoring
54 Peter on the ivories
56 "___ the season . . ."
59 "Yours, Mine and ___" (1968)
61 Occupies, as a table
65 Guitarist's purchase

68 Pelvic bones
69 Throw water on
70 Penultimate word of many fairy tales
71 "Charlotte's Web" girl
72 Subway train convenience
73 500, to a stationer

DOWN

1 Barely squeaks by (with "out")
2 Car salesman's car
3 "Don't Go ___ the Water" (1957)
4 "Her ___" (Selleck film)
5 Ice Cube film featuring a very large reptile
6 "Heartbreaker" Benatar
7 Woman of song with a "little white book"
8 Not perfect circles
9 Ambrosia go-with
10 Daiquiri ingredient
11 Peak
12 James Gandolfini's role on "The Sopranos"
13 1998 animated film
18 Partner of a promise
19 "Really?"
24 Food and shelter, for two
26 Plant swelling problem
27 Word with "face" or "chair"
28 Early stage
29 Child's "I'm innocent!"
31 "Have fun!"
33 Chronicle entry

Puzzle 14 by Mark Milhet

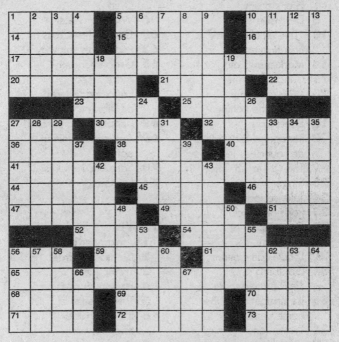

34 Busybody
35 Oft-pressed key
37 Trainees learn these
39 Africa's largest nation
42 Hoi follower
43 One who loves to take orders
48 Noises
50 "All By Myself" singer Carmen
53 Grain bane
55 Alternative
56 Comment by the work-weary

57 Gilligan's domain
58 Classic comedy, "___ Crazy"
60 San Antonio pro
62 Use a piggy bank
63 On open waters
64 Time in office
66 What Forrest Gump did for three years, five months and two days
67 Where Bruce Springsteen was born?

DRIVING LESSON

ACROSS

1 Fifer's drum
6 Defensive spray
10 "The Weakest Link" host Robinson
14 Marksman's aid
15 Unholy figurine
16 Whiskey drink
17 Begins the betting
18 Street sign
20 Item good for another go-round?
22 The "S" in T.S. Eliot
23 Singer k.d.
24 Take seriously
25 Parisian article
27 Came apart at the seams
29 Locates an aquifer
34 Goldberg and Field played them
36 It's straight from the horse's mouth
38 Brown tone
39 First shepherd
40 Per ___ (yearly)
42 Where oysters rest?
43 Series of ornamental loops
45 An option for Hamlet
46 They have a queen but no king
47 We couldn't have givers without them
49 Initials in food certification
51 Unbuttered
52 Medical suffix
54 Contained herein (Abbr.)
56 Window deicer
60 Christopher Cross hit
63 Pedestrian safeway
65 Graph heading?
66 Mare's meal
67 Prefix for "lateral" or "librium"
68 Licorice-flavored seed
69 Anti-counterfeiting agents
70 Sarcastic remarks
71 Latvians

DOWN

1 Alexander II, e.g.
2 Clearasil's target
3 Traffic jam
4 Phantom's passion
5 Take offense at
6 It's "a terrible thing to waste"
7 "Without further ___ . . ."
8 Thicket
9 Pleased as punch
10 "May I ___ silly question?"
11 Pinot ___ (dry red wine)
12 Ex-Senator Sam of Georgia
13 Divisions of joules
19 Makeovers
21 Old marketplace, in Athens
24 Abominable

Puzzle 15 by Norman S. Wizer

25 Not appropriate
26 Region from the Nile to the Red Sea
28 "___-a-Cop" (1988)
30 Friday on TV
31 Reason to slow down
32 Where to get down?
33 Cat in "Homeward Bound"
35 Fruit of the blackthorn
37 Pencil remains
41 Image-maker's tool
44 Takes a spill
48 Drunk as a skunk

50 Twenty Questions category
53 Basra native
55 "Crazy" singer
56 William Wallace, for one
57 Stuff
58 Learning by memorization
59 Part of the NAACP
60 Helicopter runners
61 Place for fresh eggs
62 Obeys the green light
64 Big brute

LOVING BEING IN LOVE

ACROSS

1 Disney dog
6 Word with "water" or "wind"
10 "___ a Lady" (Tom Jones hit)
14 More under the weather, in dialect
15 High office
16 In need of a map, maybe
17 Hudson/Day movie
19 ___ Major
20 "The ___ Who Loved Me"
21 Distress indicator
22 One who is not a cheerful giver
23 Left on board?
24 Takeout choice
26 What lovebirds may whisper to each other
30 State your address?
31 Facility
32 Black jack dealer's action
35 Throw down the gauntlet
36 Fixes, as fences
38 Plane or rail variety
39 Unusually intelligent
40 Dynamic beginning?
41 Stadium layers
42 Lovers' exchange
46 Novelty
48 Properly aged
49 Soap plant
50 Sentry's "Stop!"
51 Have a bawl
54 Mudder's father
55 What people in love see through?
58 Poor box contents
59 ___ Domini (A.D.)
60 Give the slip
61 It's more in proverbs
62 "___ there, done that"
63 Spanish title

DOWN

1 Doesn't guzzle
2 Film segment
3 Britain, to the U.S.
4 Diner owner of classic TV
5 Kick upstairs?
6 Non-computer chip?
7 Three-time U.S. Open champ Lendl
8 Musical "___ Joey"
9 Reindeer's kin
10 Turning sharply
11 Game involving ringers
12 More than a third of "Mississippi"
13 Eyeball
18 Bald, as tires
22 Selfish one's exclamation
23 Name used in exclamations
24 Neighbor of Cameroon

Puzzle 16 by Gayle Dean

25 Greeting for a villain
26 Fizzy quaff
27 End a shooting
28 Garden aerators
29 Mortise partner
33 Concerning
34 Throw casually
36 Dinner at boot camp
37 Notable times
38 ___ en scene
(stage setting)
40 "Morning Watch"
novelist
41 Pussyfoots

43 Except on the
condition
44 "Eragon" creature
45 Start to byte
46 Twangy
47 "South Pacific" hero
50 Improve, as
one's skills
51 Printer's primary color
52 Update
53 North Sea tributary
55 Talk at length
56 The loneliest number
57 Serpent's mark?

GOOD FOR THE COURSE

ACROSS

1 Some Hebrew letters
6 "The Untouchables," e.g.
10 Read quickly
14 Double-reed instruments
15 Banister, e.g.
16 Air France stopover
17 All-out effort
19 Myanmar neighbor
20 "___ Have to Do Is Dream"
21 Overthrow
22 Kindergarten supply
23 Move up the ladder
25 Baroque music luminary
26 Woodsman's tool
27 Developed favorably
31 "The ___ has landed"
34 Hardly oblivious
35 Simpson trial judge
36 Pontiac auto of song
37 Daytona 500 entry
39 Flair for music
40 It comes between the U.S. and U.K.
41 Fine-tune
42 Get into hot water?
44 Most zany
46 Chewed-up gum, e.g.
47 Clump of earth
48 Religious truths
51 "Candid Camera" man Funt
53 Talon
55 Eye membrane
57 Sauce thickener
58 Sinclair Lewis title
60 Cannes cleric
61 Vintage
62 Move in and out of traffic
63 England's "Good Queen"
64 Said three times, a liar's policy
65 Liability offsetter

DOWN

1 ___ Raton, Florida
2 Virus mentioned in 1995 film "Outbreak"
3 "For Whom the Bell ___"
4 Spiral-shaped
5 180 degrees from NNW
6 "Father of Psychoanalysis" Sigmund
7 Gobbles down
8 Gossip
9 Weaselly
10 Comfort
11 Intensive regimen for losers?
12 Gobs
13 NASDAQ alternative
18 Vanished
22 Checkout choice
24 Elbow grease
25 Actress Theda

Puzzle 17 by Lynn Lempel

27 Result of using elbow grease
28 Drudge of a writer
29 The Beehive State
30 Tiny hole in the head
31 "Goodness gracious!"
32 Princess in "A Bug's Life"
33 Woods or irons, e.g.
34 They may be seen with kings and queens
38 Bowled over
43 Regards highly
45 Emulates Mr. Universe

46 Bowls over
48 Fine partner
49 Zones
50 Holey kitchen utensil
51 Ahab, in a song
52 Part of the brain or ear
53 "Ghost Rider" star
54 Debtor's worry
56 Printer's reversal
58 Like Wonderland's Hatter
59 U.S. airline, once

LACKING COLOR

ACROSS

1 John Wayne's "___ in the Saddle"
5 To this point
10 Cradle alternative
14 Mozart's Trojan princess
15 Madrid treasure
16 "This Gun for ___"
17 Dam builder's favorite classic TV show?
20 Opposite of pencil in
21 Navigational channel
22 Type of "board" or "joint"
25 Sublease, e.g.
26 "The Garden of Earthly Delights" painter
30 One with a flat?
33 Tag line, "___ it!"
34 They may be stout
35 Sipowicz of "NYPD Blue," for one
38 Spooky TV series
42 It takes things to extremes
43 Isinglass
44 Come again, like a nightmare
45 Jazz enthusiast
47 Matzohs lack it
48 Calamari source
51 Court partitions
53 Mame and Em
56 Inclined
60 Rare utterance from Mom?
64 Smallest Great Lake, by volume
65 Contents of some closets
66 1988 U.S. Open loser to Mats
67 "Mob" or "hoop" ending
68 Manicurist's board
69 Gossip column fodder

DOWN

1 Courteney Cox series
2 Down wind, nautically
3 Half of a Jim Carrey film title
4 Substance in some lamps
5 Pitchman's speech
6 Leftover crumb
7 Like Albert of cartoons
8 Kerfuffles and foofaraws
9 Biblical attire
10 Heidi's home
11 Yankees, to the Red Sox
12 "Fame"-ous Cara
13 Picasso's headwear
18 Abstain from
19 Make money the old-fashioned way
23 Biased type?
24 State bird of Louisiana
26 Eight bits
27 Awed responses
28 Winter bird food

Puzzle 18 by Donna S. Levin

29 Computer monitor component, often
31 Nullify
32 Lenten symbol of penitence
35 Caesar's sidekick
36 Heavy responsibility
37 Saucy
39 Young scamp
40 Secret meetings
41 Zoo leader?
45 Yon partner
46 Sedgwick or Brickell
48 Yegg targets

49 Common dairy quantity
50 Loosen the laces
52 Brownish yellow
54 Perry's creator
55 Dieter's milk choice, perhaps
57 Bibliographical notation
58 Vandergelder's Dolly
59 Bolshevik quarry
61 St. Louis-to-Chicago dir.
62 Ramparts preposition
63 It does a bang-up job

AS TIME PASSES

ACROSS

1 Abs are below them
5 They're pretty and have big mouths
10 It likes the night life
13 "Once ___ a Mattress"
14 Nosegay contents, perhaps
16 Writer Bradbury
17 Clairvoyance
19 Conifer
20 Marine growth
21 Cold symptom
23 Certain billiards shot
25 Steak partner
26 Old-fashioned shoe covering
28 Revolutionary War figure
33 He's grim
35 Fashion designer Claiborne
36 Word with "folk" or "fairy"
37 Home of the Brave? (Abbr.)
38 One poking fun
41 Natal lead-in
42 Wild, desperate guess
44 Historic introduction?
45 Given new life
47 Primitive timepiece
50 Don't put this before the horse
51 England's Isle of ___
52 Henry VIII's house
54 Make suitable again
58 Locale of miraculous cures
62 "___ on a Grecian Urn"
63 Luminous coating
65 Space abode, once
66 Not a guzzler
67 "___ life!"
68 Go from ___ Z
69 Koontz and Jones
70 Shelley alma mater

DOWN

1 "___ in Boots"
2 "En garde" weapon
3 Caesar's comic partner
4 Everest topper
5 "The Sons of Katie ___" (1965)
6 Solomon's forte
7 Wallach of the silver screen
8 ___ to riches
9 Whiskered pooch
10 "Carmina Burana" composer Karl
11 Emulate a banshee
12 Ancient Greek harp
15 Nickname for Wilt Chamberlain
18 Spruce up
22 "Hot Lead and Cold ___"
24 Most balmy
26 Words before "music" or "rights"
27 Island country in the Pacific

Puzzle 19 by Diane Epperson

29 Not a whit
30 Where the lord dwells
31 Like an excellent guard dog
32 It's a gas in Las Vegas!
33 Poison ivy result
34 Type of envelope
39 Big Band ___
40 Win back
43 Raised, as racehorses
46 Onslaught
48 Sword lilies, for short
49 Long-faced

53 "Love Me Two Times" group
54 "Touched by an Angel" star Downey
55 Chop copy
56 Prefix with dynamic
57 Classify blood
59 Topic of many a New Year's resolution
60 Prefix meaning "within"
61 "___ the Man" Musial
64 Student's stat.

THE NEON LIGHTS OF . . .

ACROSS

1 Gilbert of "Roseanne"
5 Angel hair on your tongue
10 Great multitude
14 Woeful expression
15 Ali's faith
16 Stylish magazine
17 Musical featuring "I Hate Men"
19 Reached terra firma
20 Brown pigment used in drawing
21 Give credence
23 Bearded antelopes
26 "___ pig's eye!"
27 Certain Spanish gent?
33 End of a retaliatory phrase
34 Capacious
35 Oil-bearing rock
37 Winglike
39 Wear proudly
41 Preceding periods
42 Fixed the pilot?
44 Previous arrest
46 Be decisive
47 Septennial affliction?
50 Samuel's mentor
51 Where heroes come into existence?
52 Funds for the future
57 They're virtually pointless
61 Jai ___
62 Salutation for Barbie?
65 "___ Yankees"
66 A Judge, basically
67 Custard tart
68 Words with "shake" or "break"
69 Exodus commemoration
70 Temple, poetically

DOWN

1 5th Avenue store
2 What Washington couldn't tell
3 Talk like Froggy of "The Little Rascals"
4 Give, as a task
5 Horner's dessert
6 What it doesn't hurt to do
7 Croatian, e.g.
8 "Toodle-oo!"
9 Aviatrix Earhart
10 Aspirin target
11 Clay water crock
12 Narrow aperture
13 Head of France?
18 Lord's domain
22 Weekend getaway destinations, perhaps
24 Unexplained sightings
25 Slipshod
27 Virile types
28 Dickens title start
29 Martin's "That's ___"

Puzzle 20 by Ron Halverson

30 Large indefinite number

31 Widespread chaos

32 First Hebrew letter

33 Cigarette substance

36 Plus-or-minus fig.

38 Attention-grabbing

40 Moved at a good clip

43 Start for "type" or "vision"

45 Got one's dander up

48 Dark times in one's life

49 Basketball game starter

52 Nothing, somewhere

53 Israeli airline

54 "___ Time, Next Year"

55 "Sommersby" actor

56 Used a firehouse pole

58 Jazzy first name

59 Panache

60 "Auld Lang ___"

63 Light-Horse Harry

64 Hockey great Bobby

GET BEHIND ME

ACROSS

1 Collins and Donahue
6 'N Sync's Lance
10 Ty Treadway, e.g.
14 Enjoy immensely
15 Words after "Thanks"
16 Like cuttlefish defenses
17 Perfectly suited
19 Tide designation
20 Allay one's fears
21 Inclement weather provision, in a schedule
23 Word preceding "souci" or "serif"
25 Sounded like a mad dog
26 Full house indicator
29 Wets with moisture, as on grass
31 DDT banner
32 Italian resort island
34 It was once thought to be indivisible
36 Thumbs down votes
40 Montezuma, notably
41 "The Running ___" (1987)
42 2006 Scarlett Johansson film
43 Southwest tableland
44 Analyze, as evidence
45 Swahili-speaking nation
46 "Norma ___" (1979)
48 Come to grips with
50 Long, long time
51 Honored with

55 Kramden and Norton, e.g.
57 Epitome of slowness
59 Meal
63 Spinach nutrient
64 Lingering sensation
66 Full of oneself
67 Blanket choice
68 Cousteau milieu
69 Mr. of fiction
70 Keeps folks in stitches?
71 Gets warmer

DOWN

1 Anti-fur grp.
2 "Witness" actor Lukas
3 Gleason's "How sweet ___!"
4 Humdingers
5 Occurring irregularly
6 "Batman" sound effect
7 Sporting wings
8 Boston pops?
9 "Ms." magazine co-founder
10 Obstacle
11 "Love Story" star
12 Get by on thin ice?
13 Banged out
18 "In the Line of Fire" actress Russo
22 Toddler's break
24 Hindu teacher
26 Swindle
27 Bring down the house?

Puzzle 21 by Lynn Lempel

28 Stops wavering
30 Rod of Moses
33 Set up differently
35 Like some beer
37 Top-of-the-line
38 It has its ups and downs
39 Distance between pillars
42 Bare bones model?
44 They also have their ups and downs
47 Consumer bait
49 Singer Vikki

51 Folks featured in Harrison Ford's "Witness"
52 Like a bad apple
53 Audibly
54 "Robinson Crusoe" author
56 The final frontier
58 Tuck away
60 Far from land
61 General decoration
62 Teller's stack
65 Golfer from Johannesburg

16 OUNCES

ACROSS

1 "Snail mail" co.
5 Shakespearean "Bummer!"
9 Move powerlessly
14 Market oversaturation
15 Monologist after the news
16 Kukla and Fran's pal
17 POUND
20 Walk Of Fame symbols
21 Beetle Bailey's pal
22 Big bang letters
23 "Cheech & Chong's ___ Dreams" (1981)
26 Step into character
27 Felix, for one
30 POUND
36 "Baby Baby" singer
38 "Light" weapon?
39 Unhurried gait
40 Team racing event
43 Huge amount
44 Half the integers
46 Bases for movie film
48 POUND
51 AARP members
52 Logger's tool
53 Right-angled shapes
55 Verb used in recipes
58 They say the darndest things
60 Decorative toiletry cases
64 POUND
68 It sometimes needs a good paddling
69 Move like molasses
70 "This thing weighs ___!"
71 It may have a brand name
72 Danny DeVito, to Arnold Schwarzenegger (in a film)
73 Type of deal

DOWN

1 Disgusted comments
2 Part of a jukebox
3 Cougar relative
4 "Home Alone" co-star
5 Sitcom alien
6 "___ Girls" (Gene Kelly musical)
7 Animated film featuring Woody Allen's voice
8 Angry with
9 Prairie dwellers
10 Like something from the Jurassic period
11 What little things mean, in song
12 Prince's "___ 'O' The Times"
13 Run up the flagpole
18 Basketry willow
19 St. Louis landmark
24 Big shot of industry
25 Bald eagle's cousin
27 Spy in Canaan
28 "Don't make ___!" ("Freeze!")
29 Aggressive personality

Puzzle 22 by Mark Milhet

31 World record?
32 "___ Don't Preach" (hit for Madonna)
33 Brief final remarks?
34 Moray trapper
35 Lock that cannot be opened
37 Polite bloke
41 Lumbago, e.g.
42 Emulate Tarzan
45 Less sound
47 Perry of "Diary of a Mad Black woman"
49 On what the earth turns

50 More than popular
54 Word before "fast" and after "home"
55 Basics
56 "Phooey!"
57 Eat elegantly
59 Rectangular boat
61 "Do ___ others . . ."
62 Picture on a monitor
63 Last word of a holiday song title
65 Sock part
66 Israeli machine gun
67 Toon Chihuahua

CITY PLANNING

ACROSS

1 Chefs' protectors
6 It's on the watch
10 Scorch
14 Sluggish by nature
15 ___ avail (useless)
16 Approximately
17 Riser and tread, combined
18 Prefix with "China"
19 Golden rule word
20 Show stopper, often
23 "___ and ye shall find"
24 Bath powder
25 "My ___ Private Idaho" (1991)
28 Like Death's horse
30 Judd of "Taxi"
34 Bit of wampum
36 Early Briton
38 "Same here"
39 Business campuses
42 Official proclamation
43 Artsy Manhattan neighborhood
44 Champagne name
45 Vampire slayers
47 One of the Jackson 5
49 Letter addenda, for short
50 "Why don't we?"
52 General ___ chicken
54 In-home accommodations

61 "Ghostbusters" director Reitman
62 Org. with missions
63 Orderly grouping
64 Community event
65 Start of some juice names
66 Longest river in France
67 Wapitis, e.g.
68 Word on a matching towel
69 Inserted

DOWN

1 Catchall file label, briefly
2 "___ the wild blue yonder"
3 Most fans have a favorite one
4 Cuts off the ends
5 "Silkwood" star
6 Perfectionists
7 Novelist Morrison
8 Stop with
9 Do-re-mi
10 Taco topper, perhaps
11 Sea eagle
12 Hammett terrier
13 One that's cornered in chess?
21 Do a double take, e.g.

Puzzle 23 by James W. Hyres

22 Goodyear symbol
25 Some drama awards
26 "Cheers" actor
27 Gymnast Comaneci
29 "Cats" T.S.
31 Razor sharpener
32 Some soft drinks
33 Emcees
35 Young swimmers
37 Some French Polynesians
40 Fine horse

41 "___ luck!"
46 Foul fetor
48 "C'est magnifique!"
51 Kind of drum
53 New England seafood
54 "All ___!" (court phrase)
55 Mean business?
56 Made, as a putt
57 Bygone autocrat
58 Dry as a bone
59 Infrequent
60 Got a load of

COBBLING

ACROSS

1 Pertaining to birth
6 Play, as a mandolin
11 "Dear old" fellow
14 Come to light
15 Rib
16 Poetic work
17 Morale booster
19 Prevail
20 Be bratty, in a way
21 Club leader?
22 You may switch them
24 Deliverer of deceit
28 Evolve into
31 Old TV series "The ___ Limits"
32 "Asteroids" game creator
33 You may part with it
35 Hamper contents
38 Beetle juice?
39 Chapel Hill sports fan
42 The Righteous Brothers, e.g.
43 Do in, as a dragon
45 She was wild about Harry
46 Leads the bidding
48 Greeted the queen
50 Thick, messy substance
51 Seafood selection
55 Plumber's tool
56 Broadcasting band, briefly ___
57 Tell all
61 Gymnastics feat
62 Brussels souvenir
66 "The Two Towers" monster
67 Become slippery, in a way
68 Prosperous times
69 NEA ally
70 Large bags
71 Worthwhile thing

DOWN

1 Kindergarten breaks
2 "Fidelio" song
3 Involuntary movements
4 Requests
5 "Crooklyn" director Spike
6 In a rut
7 House with a smoke hole
8 Jay-Z's genre
9 Function
10 Red wine
11 Demoted
12 Parting word
13 Concentrated
18 Few and far between
23 Over again
25 Fail to mention
26 Gable alternatives
27 Boob ___ (television)
28 Redcap's burden

Puzzle 24 by Lynn Lempel

29 List ender
30 1942 film classic
33 Statement of belief
34 Words of surprise
36 Crooned
37 Fire engine staple
40 Help
41 Lounge around
44 The sunny side,
  in sunny side up
47 Adobe villages
49 Tad
50 Parlor piece
51 Camera setting

52 Unresponsive
53 Multi-voice
  composition
54 They may pass
  in the night
58 Ho Chi Minh
  Trail locale
59 Vertex
60 Brief letter
  sign-off
63 Logical start?
64 Authorize
65 Org. with
  a lottery

WATCH THE BIRDIE

ACROSS

1 Common computer font
6 Big "first" for baby
10 Very plentiful
14 Electrical pioneer Nikola
15 Lime cover
16 Egg without a shell
17 Brother on a noted TV sitcom
19 Source of misery
20 Poem of devotion
21 Swarm
22 Sudden emotional pang
24 Like Death's horse
25 Feature of Colorado
26 Jellied side dishes
29 Outlet insert
30 Searched for bugs
31 "The Ghost and Mrs. ___"
32 Rival of Bjorn
36 "___ on Down the Road"
37 Jazz legend Chick
38 Be a peddler
39 Holiday cherub
40 French articles
41 Desist partner
42 Informal farewell
44 Trust in
45 "Titanic" or "Star Wars," e.g.
48 Old salts
49 Maltreatment
50 Repeated word in a Doris Day tune
51 Stable tidbit
54 Word repeated before "pants on fire"
55 "Network" actor
58 Town in Italy, New Jersey or California
59 Shah's domain, once
60 One in charge of a roast?
61 Suit to ___
62 Brain scans, for short
63 Type of whale

DOWN

1 "___ cost to you!"
2 He played Flytrap on "WKRP in Cincinnati"
3 ". . . here on Gilligan's ___"
4 "Cakes and ___" (Maugham)
5 The end for playwrights?
6 Buying binge
7 "The Dream ___" (1989)
8 Velvet end?
9 Overabundance
10 "A Rage in Harlem" actress
11 Marla's predecessor
12 Toadstools and mushrooms, e.g.
13 Middle East prince
18 Some Disney collectibles

Puzzle 25 by Elizabeth C. Gorski

23 Lose or draw
   alternative
24 "Carrie" actress
25 Makes an effort
26 Whaling, e.g.
27 Dog-paddled, e.g.
28 Item for a Mexican pot?
29 Less sullied
31 "Haystacks" artist
33 Job for Mr. Fixit
34 Start of many words?
35 Ancient garden
   location
37 Attractive one

41 Wide-mouthed servers
43 Patient replies?
44 Roseanne, formerly
45 Actress Jovovich
46 T.S. or George
47 Forest clearing
48 They're coming of age
50 Deer fellow?
51 "___ Upon a
   Honeymoon" (1942)
52 Serving standout
53 1954 horror classic
56 ". . . ___ I saw Elba"
57 Young mischief-maker

FAR OFF PLACES

ACROSS

1 Wheelchair access
5 Squad car
9 People with their pants on fire?
14 It may be "restricted" on a military base
15 Badgered
16 Laurel's nickname for Hardy
17 Point of departure
20 "My Cherie ___" (Stevie Wonder song)
21 Pueblo crockpot
22 "___ Cars" (1980)
23 Sinatra's Gardner
25 "The Defiant ___" (Poitier film)
27 Place of disappearance
34 Sherlock's Blue Carbuncle, for one
35 Within shouting distance
36 Golfer with an "army"
37 Up in years
39 Preferred invitees
42 Strong desires
43 Overpowering terror
45 "Little ___ of Horrors"
47 Barnum and 109, e.g.
48 Impossibly distant places
52 Epps of "Love and Basketball"
53 Where fat cats get less fat
54 ". . . happily ___ after"
57 Bygone big birds
60 Posed a question
64 Timbuktu
67 Drama of Euripides
68 Boat's bow
69 Like some proportions
70 Clio, Edgar, Hugo, Oscar or Tony
71 Planted
72 Where you may skate on thin ice

DOWN

1 Indian prince
2 Calla lily, e.g.
3 Short office note
4 New Guinea native
5 Mantel piece
6 NASA scratch
7 "American ___" (music show)
8 Non-stick coating
9 Cut off, as branches
10 Not what it appears to be
11 Lament for "poor Yorick"
12 Dish sometimes made in a minute
13 It's for the birds
18 Baseball Hall of Famer Monte
19 Diller's spouse, affectionately
24 On the ocean
26 Org. that controls emissions
27 Meat avoider
28 Square things?
29 Holbrook of "The Firm"
30 "My Wild ___ Rose"
31 All thumbs
32 Final Beethoven symphony

Puzzle 26 by Gayle Dean

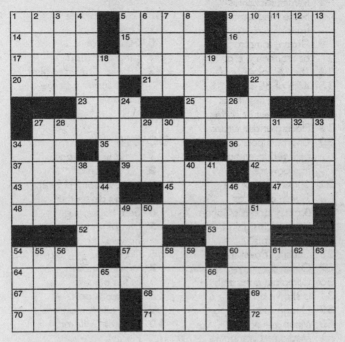

33 "___ of the d'Urbervilles"
34 Open-mouthed stare
38 Chaos
40 "___ Believes in Me"
41 Little piggies?
44 Internet address ending, typically
46 Southern fruit tree
49 Irene Cara hit film
50 Cavalry units
51 Serving of bacon
54 Thompson in "Dead Again"

55 "Room With a ___"
56 Scandinavian literary collection
58 Hendrix hairstyle
59 "___ Falling on Cedars" (1999)
61 French soldier's cap
62 "___ Brockovich" (2000 film)
63 Where to find two black suits
65 Terhune's "___: a Dog"
66 "A League of Their ___"

VEILED THREAT

ACROSS

1 Munch munchies
5 Some Mediterranean fruits
9 Grape, tomato or cranberry, e.g.
14 The "A" of ABM
15 45th of 50 states
16 Divest of munitions
17 Kind of tea or coffee
18 Placing under wraps
20 Charm superstitiously believed to embody magical powers
22 12th month of the Jewish calendar
23 Bradley and McMahon
24 Voyager insignia
26 DEA agents
28 Chasing down flies
32 Out-of-the-way
36 Complain constantly
37 Is shown on TV
39 "Judge Judy" supply
40 Moon valley
41 Medicated compress
43 Daily Planet reporter
44 "The ___" (series starring Mr. T)
46 Word of hearty concurrence
47 Carefree quality
48 Chopped finely
50 Diocese subdivisions
52 Bahrain bigwig
54 Campus marchers (Abbr.)
55 Informal affirmative
58 Road Runner's sound
60 Hardy, vis-a-vis Laurel
64 Anonymous social

67 Newsstand purchase, perhaps
68 Town employee of yore
69 Herbal do-all
70 Slippery ones
71 King and Ladd
72 "The ___" (Midler film)
73 "One Flew Over the Cuckoo's ___"

DOWN

1 Babe in the woods
2 "___ Upon a Honeymoon" (1942)
3 "Don't delete this"
4 Safe house, e.g.
5 Shrubs with purplish flowers
6 "How was ___ know?"
7 What you did at the office?
8 Bookcase part
9 Real-estate magnate
10 Blyth of "Mildred Pierce"
11 Pet store purchase
12 Gunk
13 Word on a fuse
19 "Shoulda, woulda, coulda" thinker
21 Problem of the middle ages?
25 Soul singer Baker
27 It's used to conceal actual plans
28 "Vamoose!"
29 Duvalier's domain, once
30 "Over the Rainbow" composer

Puzzle 27 by Ron Halverson

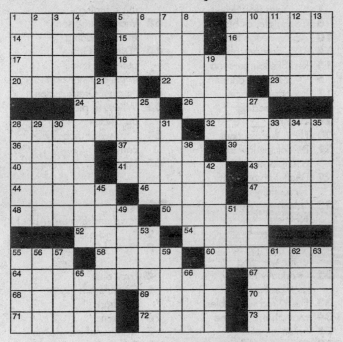

31 Jack Lemmon role in '93 and '95
33 West Indian witchcraft
34 It may be past, present or future
35 Bass-baritone Simon
38 Mammoth hunter's weapon
42 Register signer
45 Country club attendees
49 Gave up the ghost
51 "Let's call ___ day"
53 Reinforcement for concrete

55 Village People hit
56 Jazzman ___ "Fatha" Hines
57 Home to many Indians, but few cowboys
59 ___ Alto, Calif.
61 Open delight
62 90-degree shapes
63 Indication to stop playing
65 Documentary filmmaker Burns
66 Part of UCLA

WEDDING DAY

ACROSS

1. ___ Yello (soft drink)
6. Coagulate, as blood
10. Acknowledge frankly
14. "___ Caesar's ghost!"
15. Red Skelton persona
16. Over-the-top anger
17. Important person at the wedding
19. "Winnie ___ Pu"
20. Fly in the ointment
21. Part of the lowest possible straight
22. Dealt with adversity successfully
23. "Much ___ About Nothing"
25. Prayer beads
26. Important person at the wedding
32. Gradually destroy, as shoreline
33. Fleshy red vegetables
34. Matterhorn, for one
37. Salon supplies
38. "Beauty and the Beast" beauty
39. Wedding cake layer
40. "Do the Right Thing" pizzeria owner
41. Strong cotton thread
42. Naples noodle dish
43. Important people at the wedding
46. Black or ruffed bird
48. Rowboat accessory
49. Chick's hangout?
50. Pizzazz
53. Extras in "2001: A Space Odyssey"
57. They are six in an inning
58. Important person at the wedding
60. "Days of Grace" author Arthur
61. It has a Minor part
62. Ancient Greek region
63. Where to pick up chicks?
64. ". . . which nobody can ___"
65. Beginning

DOWN

1. Torre and Stengel (Abbr.)
2. "___ go bragh!"
3. "Love Me or Leave Me" singer Horne
4. Lazy ones
5. Gambler's hangout, for short
6. Blacken
7. Traditional knowledge
8. Follow orders
9. Rocky hill
10. Melodic composition
11. Chief Chilean port
12. One concerned with figures?
13. Like a neglected garden
18. City on the Thames
22. Joint tenants?
24. Pseudonymous surname
25. Mechanical learning method
26. Actresses Ryan and Tilly
27. Word with "code" or "rug"

28 Places for coin collectors?
29 Tipping the scales
30 Loesser musical "The Most Happy ___"
31 Face that "launched a thousand ships"
35 Mother of Apollo
36 Hyde Park stroller
38 ___ one's time
39 Bitter green herb
41 "Schindler's ___"
42 Certain tour operator, briefly
44 Kind of potato

45 "Finished!"
46 Response to a weak joke
47 Shake awake
50 "If all ___ fails . . ."
51 Type of cloth
52 "___ in a Manger"
54 Word with "bobby" and "bowling"
55 One of a watery quintet
56 Bedframe crosspiece
58 Beanie Babies or the Hula-Hoop, e.g.
59 "___ Bravo" (John Wayne film)

STEP LIVELY

ACROSS

1 Carson's "Tonight Show" predecessor
5 Freeze front?
9 One who keeps things kosher
14 Scots-Gaelic
15 Rimini of "The King of Queens"
16 Sweater synthetic
17 Step out
20 Used the VCR
21 "___-12" (police drama)
22 Pursue with passion
23 Petri-dish gel
26 Pin the ___ on the donkey
28 Step in
34 Words with "roll" or "tear"
35 Check for letters?
36 Electric surge
38 Entrance for Clementine's dad
40 Afternoon TV shows
43 One type of poll
44 Administered medicine
46 Hockey shot
48 Hudson Bay prov.
49 Step up
53 Luminous topper
54 Warm, in searches
55 Tour operator
58 Hindu royal
60 "Falcon ___"
64 Step down
68 Bridge bid, briefly
69 Pelvic bones
70 It keeps on rolling
71 "___ By Me" (film directed by Rob Reiner)
72 Depend (on)
73 Fit to finish?

DOWN

1 Animal's skin
2 Word with "disaster" or "dining"
3 Word on an urgent message
4 Make public
5 Cat fancier from Melmac
6 Prefix with "classical" or "conservative"
7 Butler's quarters?
8 "There was no other choice for me!"
9 Co-renters, slangily
10 Escort's offering
11 "Honey, I ___ Up The Kid" (1992)
12 Lead singer of U2
13 "___ the wild blue yonder"
18 Ex FBI boss, ___ J Hoover
19 "Just the facts, ___"
24 Blackjack components
25 City near Lake Tahoe
27 Bounding gait
28 Caldwell's "Tobacco ___"
29 Words with "the line" or "an era"
30 Rupee part
31 Store secretly
32 Watergate figure

33 Barely making (with "out")
37 Kitchen extension?
39 Word in many college names
41 It may be hatched
42 Ad come-on
45 1996 Greg Kinnear film
47 "Melrose ___"
50 Rickman of "Galaxy Quest"
51 Nicolas Cage film of '97

52 Novel flubs
55 Advantages
56 Polite bloke
57 In midvoyage
59 Cruise stopover, perhaps
61 Shorten to fit, perhaps
62 Parched
63 It may have a knot in it
65 Setting for "Newhart"
66 Feel unwell
67 Hen's task

CLEAR AS A BELL

ACROSS

1 Tireless carrier
5 Landed
9 Fervidness
14 Poi, essentially
15 "Gone With the Wind" mansion
16 Regional animals
17 Straightforward
20 Frank McCourt sequel
21 Appearance
22 Card catalogue entries
23 Shish kebab necessity
25 Civil rights worker Medgar
27 "The Defiant ___" (1958)
29 "A Nightmare on ___ Street"
30 Feature of David Letterman's smile
33 Young cod
36 Viscount's superior
38 "Black Beauty" author Sewell
39 Straightforward
42 Party servers
43 "___ in America"
44 Genesis
45 Hold out one's paw?
46 Parked oneself
47 Homestead's county
49 Light sleeper
51 Peruse again
55 Part of F.D.R.
58 PC screen image
60 Born
61 Straightforward
64 Jerk one's knee, perhaps
65 Picked-on instruments, for short
66 Basic bit
67 Jason's wife, in myth
68 Jane of literature
69 Invigorates (with "up")

DOWN

1 Box score data
2 Corrective eye surgery
3 Demagnetize, as a tape
4 Joltin' Joe's bro
5 It suits you
6 Type of edition
7 Castle with many steps?
8 Feather bed?
9 Maintain to be true
10 Balsa vessels, e.g.
11 Type of citizenship
12 "___ Upon a Mattress" (play starring Carol Burnett)
13 "Willard" creatures
18 Changes, as the Constitution
19 1887 Verdi opera
24 Low barks
26 Knowledgeable
28 Group with a lot of bills

Puzzle 30 by Gayle Dean

30 Black wildebeests
31 Cost for a deal?
32 Bygone era
33 Give the brush-off
34 Place for seeds
35 Bilbo Baggins' find
37 Explain further
38 Dogpatch denizen
40 Large, powerful woman
41 Gnawing mammal
46 Musical composition
48 Wake from sleep

49 David Bowie hit "Let's ___"
50 Daring
52 Descended on the mother's side
53 Fabulous fabulist
54 Judges to be
55 Campus quarters
56 Fencing tool
57 Take charge on the dance floor
59 A Witch of Eastwick
62 Expected
63 Toy gun ammo

TIME FOR CHANGE

ACROSS

1 Midnight cash sources
5 They're swollen on some superstars
9 Showy success
14 Hat's edge
15 Hunky-___
16 Vestige
17 Trashy paperback
19 This puzzle's theme
20 Be of service
21 Hush-hush
23 Vampire in a Rice title
25 Primitive home
26 Protection around the lungs
29 Exhortation for a panicky person
34 One-named Nigerian singer
38 "Nutty" bird
40 Scalawag
41 Certain U.S. Open figure
44 Tuck of fiction
45 Babushka
46 Pot foundation
47 Mortarboard part
49 Blacksmith's tool
51 Radial fill
53 Docile creatures
58 It has its ups and downs
64 Bond or Smiley
65 Dictator's asst.
66 Beatles hit
68 Unintended spot
69 Peter Fonda role
70 Canal of renown
71 Law school subjects
72 Type of bargain
73 Asian unit of weight

DOWN

1 Paula of "American Idol"
2 Played out
3 Rogers and Drew Carey's TV foil
4 Silvery food fish
5 Tokyo, long ago
6 U.S. bureaucracy
7 Popular cookie snack
8 Slender, graceful woman
9 "Yadda, yadda, yadda"
10 "Peter Pan" creature
11 Bestial hideaway
12 Result of surplus oil?
13 Sound engineer's word
18 Word with "miss" or "catastrophe"
22 "Red October," for one
24 Bathroom wall-covering, often
27 "___ on the Fourth of July"
28 Yet
30 Popular beverage
31 Once more, Dogpatch-style
32 A deadly sin
33 Distribute (with "out")

Puzzle 31 by Elizabeth C. Gorski

34 Architect's meas.

35 That certain something

36 Lectern platform

37 Important times in history

39 1492 ship

42 High crimes

43 Former soccer org. Pele once played in

48 Three sheets to the wind

50 It's staged

52 Tear to shreds

54 Shoelace thingamajig

55 Stiller and ___

56 Vanity Fair photographer Leibovitz

57 "___ Magnolias"

58 "You there"

59 "Beetle Bailey" canine

60 Paraphernalia

61 Words with "step" or "sleep"

62 Perp's place

63 Anterior cruciate ligament joint

67 Orchestra's funding org., perhaps

TRASH PICKUP

ACROSS

1 Sounds from the cote
5 Hammett's sleuth
10 Like some orders
14 "I'm ___ here!"
15 UFO passenger
16 Ersatz butter
17 "Now hear this!" (Abbr.)
18 Bumps on a branch
19 Gender abbreviation
20 Litter
23 Wasn't used
24 "Electric" fish
25 Recruit's sentence ender
28 Anchor store locale
31 "Analyze This" star
36 "Hard Hearted Hannah" co-composer
38 Classic motorcars
40 Arctic duck
41 Litter
44 Lloyd Webber show
45 Oliver's co-star
46 Fair to middling
47 Hinder progress
49 Sound from a sewing circle
51 Gymnast's reward
52 Air show formation
54 Airline ticket word, sometimes
56 Litter
65 "The Vampire Lestat" author
66 Heavenly space
67 "A ___ bagatelle!"
68 Dustups
69 Baby Moses was hidden among them
70 Ireland, romantically
71 It's rigged
72 Needing kneading
73 Splinter group

DOWN

1 Wild swine
2 Biographical beginning?
3 Princess in "A Bug's Life"
4 "___ of Iwo Jima" (1949 film)
5 Free from pathogens
6 Walk with weariness
7 Man Friday
8 "Nothing runs like a ___"
9 Followed
10 Grant's landmark
11 Jai ___
12 With a discount of
13 Scottish lake
21 Uncle in a top hat
22 Censor's insertion
25 Not so chancy
26 "___ at the office"
27 "Please ___" (invoice stamp)
29 Ones born in late July
30 Some Soho digs
32 Beats by a nose
33 Word with "savant" or "proof"

Puzzle 32 by Ron Halverson

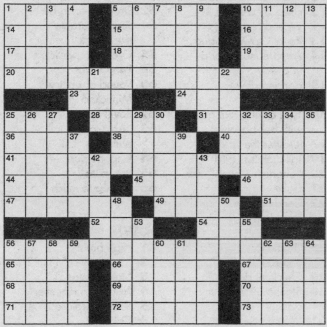

34 Cooperstown
Pee Wee
35 First name in
film directing
37 "Educating ___"
(1983 film)
39 Bridge length
42 Metamorphosis
candidate
43 It's vast
48 Gobi, for one
50 Poe setting
53 First name
in cosmetics

55 Pinnacles
56 Hit the books hard
57 Leontyne
Price role
58 Sergeants and
corporals, e.g.
59 Optional part
of a suit
60 Afterward
61 Beatty film
62 Where the
buck stops?
63 "Red" Viking
64 It's overhead

WAIST MANAGEMENT

ACROSS
1 Place for a keystone
5 Fitted by a smith
9 Wound remnant
13 Royal Crown product
14 Prepare mushrooms, in a way
15 Handed-down knowledge
16 Type of ring that goes with bell-bottoms
17 It settles the score
19 Tall flightless bird
20 "Charlie's Angels" star
21 Gully
22 Condescend
24 "Into Thin ___" (1985)
25 "I hate to ___ and run"
26 Checkout device
30 Sigourney Weaver classic
31 Woman treated as an object?
32 California campus
36 "Bonnie and Clyde" director
37 Type of semiconductor
39 Part of Indochina
40 Indiscriminating hirers, initially
41 "Da Ya Think I'm Sexy?" singer Stewart
42 "Father of Impressionism"
43 Darth Vader foe
47 Briquette remnant
50 Romans' caviar
51 From a certain grain
52 Drop off for a bit
54 Jimmy Durante trademark
55 Cyclotron particle
58 Pane frame
60 Pound of poetry
61 Mimicked
62 Bewildered
63 "Able to ___ tall buildings . . ."
64 Capone pursuer
65 Pro votes
66 Not up to much

DOWN
1 High point
2 "___ Service" (1992)
3 State of bliss
4 "If I ___ a Hammer"
5 Verbally refused
6 Colored
7 Racetrack alternative, briefly
8 Backside
9 Ukrainian, e.g.
10 Commentator Roberts
11 Site for Globetrotters
12 Che Guevara attire
14 Stiffly theatrical
18 Doo-wop classic "Duke of ___"
20 Lender's backup
23 Still
24 Reading position, sometimes

Puzzle 33 by Lynn Lempel

26 Attire for the Headless Horseman
27 "The low-priced spread"
28 TV's Morgenstern
29 Green Wave school
33 Given sainthood
34 Client for Clarence Darrow
35 Piedmont province
37 Off-street parking area
38 Hawkeye State
42 Apportion
44 Clown of early TV

45 Lasso loops
46 Buckwheat cereal
47 Dam extending across the Nile
48 Take potshots
49 Sharpens, as skills
53 "Against All ___"
54 Space Age org.
56 Type of surgeon
57 Mane spot
59 ___ Anne de Bellevue, Que.
60 Wallach of "The Magnificent Seven"

MORE, MORE, MORE

ACROSS

1 Beatnik's digs
4 Make tracks
9 Hello, somewhere in the U.S.
14 Snoopy, in his fantasies
15 Gladiator workplace
16 Got by with difficulty
17 Herd mentality
20 Biscuitlike quick bread
21 Color of the inexperienced?
22 Feeder frequenter
23 Members of a secret order
26 Backing
29 Thanksgiving serving
30 Many have comfortable seats
31 Light meal
32 Inner tube?
33 Tick or mite, e.g.
35 Democracy result
38 Yellow shade
39 Metrical units
40 Lab culture gel
41 Tree trunks
42 Drive-thru feature, perhaps
45 It means nothing
46 Fished with a net
48 Folklore monster
49 Makes oneself heard
51 Where to find irises
52 Epic extras
57 Able to be drawn

58 Course of travel
59 "Look at Me, I'm Sandra ___"
60 Cafe au lait holder
61 "Animal House" moniker
62 Check the check

DOWN

1 Ignore, as a stranger on the street
2 Australia's national blossom
3 Misshape
4 Stuff to the gills
5 Use leverage
6 Gift in Maui
7 Home away from home, perhaps
8 Dramatic dances
9 High spots
10 Brain or ear area
11 Start a barrage
12 Possessive pronoun
13 Many are personal
18 Wind up
19 Vase with a footed base
23 Join in wedlock
24 Dissenter's position
25 Network component
27 Sheriff Taylor saved him a place
28 Type of meat or pepper
30 Very out of pocket
31 Indonesian island

Puzzle 34 by Diane C. Baldwin

32 Open a little
33 Fortified
34 World Series winners of 1908
35 Gift-givers, in an O. Henry story
36 Data scrutinizers
37 Clinton alma mater
38 Six-pack component
41 Informal eating place
42 It may be hidden
43 Gave and got
44 Made a shambles of (with "up")

46 It's not on the level
47 North Pole denizen
48 Gametes
50 Cockpit guesses, for short
51 Mouse manipulator
52 Item in a tent, perhaps
53 Collection of anecdotes, e.g.
54 Currently popular
55 It's said with a thumb in the air
56 Shoshone

RISE UP

ACROSS
1 Pet protector, for short
5 Skyrockets
10 Business address abbr.
13 Miami team
14 Inuit's abode
15 It's got you covered
16 Alice's chronicler, in song
17 Play up to the audience
19 Tonic water ingredients
21 Itty-bitty bits
22 Epochs
23 Gush out
25 "___ Fear" (Gere/Norton film)
28 Out-of-favor apple treatment
29 123-45-6789, e.g. (Abbr.)
32 Homeowner's hangover?
33 Bouquet
35 Movement leaders
38 Carries on
39 Potatoes partner
40 Words with "jam" or "hurry"
41 Related by blood
42 Causes concern
44 Wood strip
45 "They ___ With Their Boots On" (1941 film)
46 Point in question
49 Town assemblies
53 Total cessation
56 Kinks' lady of song
57 When doubled, a celebrated panda
58 Exhibit's backer?
59 Vientiane locale
60 Before, in sonnets
61 Formula of belief
62 Resistance units

DOWN
1 "Kazaam" star, familiarly
2 Lima's land
3 City and drug cartel in Colombia
4 Compensation for a wrong
5 Radio transmission
6 Frightful giants
7 "Ah, me!"
8 "Apollo 13" director Howard
9 Nursery offering
10 Game for those with less than a full deck
11 Frank's daughter
12 Brings to a close
15 Place in a hold
18 Rugged mountain range
20 CPA's suggestion
23 Quarry units
24 One for the books
25 "With Honors" actor
26 Boca ___
27 Mrs. Trump, once

Puzzle 35 by Ron Halverson

28 Shakespearean forest
29 Scrooge's expression
30 "Take a powder"
31 Termitaria, e.g.
33 It may be forbidden
34 Bony-plated beast
36 Placed a call
37 "(You're) Having My Baby" singer
42 "Do the Right Thing" actor
43 Net judge's call

44 "Song ___ Blue" (Neil Diamond hit)
45 Struck out, editorially
46 Seagirt land
47 Get it all together?
48 Not certifiable
49 ___ en scene (stage setting)
50 Father of Ham
51 Grab, slangily
52 Lip service
54 Wall St. police
55 Feather partner

COMMAND PERFORMANCE

ACROSS

1 Fastening device
6 Fly-by-night
11 Buck Rogers portrayer Gerard
14 Live to ___ old age
15 Netherlands seat of government (with "The")
16 A Gabor
17 Become ruined
19 Pop top
20 Safeguard
21 Teamwork deterrent
22 Sicilian volcano
23 "All My Children" and others
25 Jazz fan?
27 Mother Costanza, on "Seinfeld"
30 "New York ___ of Mind"
31 "___ For Two"
32 D-Day town
34 Keep the auction going
37 Sulu of classic TV
40 La's lead-in
41 Battery terminal
42 Words with "bend" or "lend"
43 "Indeed!" overseas
45 Grand ___ Opry
46 Large land area
48 Part of a convenience store
51 The Parthenon is dedicated to her

53 Conserve, in a way
54 Told a story
55 Fifth day of Kwanzaa
57 Tower Bridge river
61 Seaman
62 Do it anyway
64 Man-mouse link
65 Hit musical and film
66 A bit of antiquity
67 Gullible one
68 Pine product
69 Noisy inhalation

DOWN

1 "City of Angels" star
2 "Battlefield Earth" author Hubbard
3 British isles
4 Blondie, to Dagwood
5 Gas, in Greenwich
6 Eve was the first
7 God of the underworld
8 Very excited
9 Indian canoe or baseball field structure
10 Survey choice, perhaps
11 Be dismissed
12 Donald's ex
13 Father of Rachel and Leah
18 Gets better
22 What most baked goods are?
24 Mind the pooch, in a way

Puzzle 36 by Robert H. Wolfe

26 Skating star Lipinski
27 Singer James
28 First name in
Bond portrayers
29 Accept blame
30 Comfort
33 Part of UCLA
35 Kind of chatter
36 Big bucks?
38 Like some seals
39 Neighbor of
Turkmenistan
44 Early part of life
47 Certain tooth

49 Ballpark figures
50 Spruce up
51 Some choristers
52 Papal headgear
53 Diameter
fractions
56 Places to stay
58 Otis' pal, in film
59 Eastern title
60 Faction
62 Where successful
people go?
63 Word that has
ended many fights

POSE FOR A PORTRAIT

ACROSS

1 Type of milk
5 More, to minimalists
9 Relieve of weapons
14 You're out unless you put this in
15 Differential-gear locale
16 Salk's conquest
17 Run wild
19 Native of Peru
20 Touch lightly in passing
22 Some like it felt
23 Beehive State tribesman
24 Maternally related
28 "It Wasn't All Velvet" autobiographer
31 "Spring forward" letters
34 It became independent in 1821
36 Place to find a porter
37 Its tail flaps in the wind
38 Party hearty
41 It's supportive for those eating in bed
42 Start of the Lord's Prayer
43 Encircled and attacked
44 Fashion monogram
45 Lose one's mind
47 In the poorhouse
48 Music scale note
49 Former name of Tokyo
51 Brilliant idea
59 Sports complex
60 Group of street musicians from 34-Across

62 Clerk of the 4077th
63 Midmonth day
64 Foreign currency
65 To the left, to sailors
66 Abound
67 Tool repository

DOWN

1 Mattress problem
2 Tuning device
3 "Ripley's Believe ___ not!"
4 Mouth-watering reading material
5 Shaping machine
6 Old-fashioned stage direction
7 Prelude to a duel
8 Word sung by Doris Day
9 Awake into the wee hours
10 "Honest!"
11 Alda of "M*A*S*H"
12 Custom auto accessories
13 Castle defense
18 Facet
21 Cajun concoctions
24 E, on a gas gauge
25 Closes in on
26 Located around a central hub
27 Like Ho's bubbles
29 Reason to buy Met tickets

30 Same old grind
31 Mournful melody
32 One of "The Avengers"
33 White House nickname
35 "My Favorite Year" star
37 Cap site
39 What you want your car engine to do
40 Ryder of Tinseltown
45 Racing vehicle
46 Extent

48 Coast Guard equipment
50 Certain religious philosophy
51 "___ Smile" (Hall and Oates)
52 Links hazard
53 More than patch up
54 Leave unsaid
55 Age blue jeans
56 Cold confections
57 "Nope"
58 Mudder's father
61 Turf

NEW AND IMPROVED

ACROSS

1 "East of ___"
5 Speaker go-with
8 Co-Nobelist with Begin
13 "I Just Wanna Stop" singer Vannelli
14 Remarkable deed
16 TV time that begins in the evening
17 Deserves a slap, perhaps
19 Red Square mausoleum occupant
20 Have the same views
21 "Take This Job and ___ It"
23 Carbon-14 determination
24 "Hee Haw" banjoist Clark
25 Right from the oven
28 Net gains?
30 End of a college address
31 Existed
33 "The Drew Carey Show" setting
37 Desert spot
41 It flows through a conductor
44 English test, perhaps
45 Four-footed friends
46 "Wayne's World" star Carvey
47 Gym alternative
49 "Hey there"
51 "Not a minute afterward"

57 Contemptible fellow
60 Encouraging word
61 "Is that your ___ answer?"
62 Idolize
64 What the fat lady sings
66 One-time paperback
68 Combat doctor
69 "Call of the Wild" vehicle
70 Melodious Horne
71 Condensed but memorable saying
72 Some NCAA basketball players
73 Carhop's load

DOWN

1 British actress Samantha
2 Mexican artist Rivera
3 Contestants' costs
4 Race-winning margin, sometimes
5 Neighbor of Eur.
6 Reagan attorney general
7 Ottoman official
8 Display of grandeur
9 "Butterflies ___ Free"
10 Talk-show hostess Shore
11 Southwest sidekick
12 Group principle
15 Shoe man McCann
18 Parker of "Old Yeller"
22 Go for the gold
26 Thursday is named for him

27 Property protectors
29 One way to pay
31 Quilters' get-together
32 Singh rival
34 Place to shoot from
35 It may be crushed
36 World Series mo.
38 Auto sprucer-upper
39 Country lodging
40 RR stop
42 Word processing
decision
43 Org. that delivers
the goods

48 Clay, today
50 Cutup with Oliver
51 Fragrance
52 For later viewing
53 Screen vixen Bara
54 Sentence joiners
55 Coin toss choice
56 Glue name
58 "Gladiator" setting
59 Postponement
63 Numskull
65 Predetermine
the outcome
67 Sullivan and Koch

BARELY PASSING GRADES

ACROSS

1 Roach and Linden
5 Acts as lookout, e.g.
10 Pt. of IRA
14 Genesis hunter
15 Camp David accords participant
16 Ayatollah's predecessor
17 "Answer, please" (Abbr.)
18 Poppycock
19 Fillable bread
20 1978 Best Picture (with "The")
22 The "dismal science," for short
23 Wall and Easy
24 Noise from the farm
26 Vivacious actress West
27 Barbecue rod
29 Bowlike curve
32 ___ d'art
35 Rosary items
36 Arrived lifeless, briefly
37 Plain of Jars locale
38 Loads the hook
39 "___ Window"
40 Tough wood
41 It may be grand
42 Watering hole items
43 Boggy area
44 Dover specialty
45 X-ray unit
46 Raw information
48 Dunce
52 "Bullets" in poker
54 Period of suspended activity
57 Needle apertures
58 Sing the praises of
59 In ___ (bored with things)
60 One in a million
61 Wheel brace
62 Like some circumstances
63 Addition column
64 Chromatic nuances
65 Divination practitioner

DOWN

1 Flocks
2 Rainy day need
3 Four-time Wimbledon champ Rod
4 Classic Motown group (with "The")
5 On the ball
6 Sights in the country
7 Prepare for publication
8 Word with "deck" or "measure"
9 Banned NFL substances
10 Forest quaker
11 Word in a W.C. Fields film title
12 "The Elder" of history
13 "Better you ___ me!"
21 Kind of wave
25 Part of TGIF
27 Take by force

Puzzle 39 by Ron Halverson

28 Fancy chopped liver
30 Laugh heartily
31 What some plants produce
32 Patron saint of Norway
33 Bag of diamonds?
34 Plow pioneer
35 What some people jump
38 With the most breadth
39 Lucille Ball and many others
41 Western time

42 Roseanne, before Tom
45 Searches through
47 Hinny and ninny, e.g.
48 Pig in ___
49 Ghastly strange
50 Color of a clear sky
51 Dissuade
52 Aviation prefix
53 Primary color in photography
55 Public art show or former Montreal athlete
56 British school

ROUTINE BUSINESS

ACROSS

1 Frolicking run
5 Barber's belt
10 Go against
14 "Dukes of Hazard" character
15 Canonized 2nd-century pope
16 "Buck" attachment
17 The "Three" of a classic TV title
18 Easygoing dude
20 Hambletonian race entrants
22 Matador's foe, in Madrid
23 Boathouse item
24 "Take Me ___ to the Ballgame"
25 Canine called Fifi, in stereotypes
33 A star stands for it
34 Dog tags, e.g.
35 Locale of Hitchcock's window
36 "The Last Picture Show" locale
37 Booker T. and the ___
38 Hayes of the Basketball Hall of Fame
39 Suggestive look
40 Engineer's place
41 Halfpennies, e.g.
42 Oscar-winning film directed by Robert Redford
46 Classified items
47 More than most

48 Conceive a notion
52 Providing essential information
57 Bad thing to catch
59 Opera solo
60 Boob tube award
61 Camp craft
62 Hang around
63 London get-togethers
64 Fancy-shmancy pitchers
65 Pant part

DOWN

1 "The ___ is history"
2 ___ about (approximately)
3 Stereo precursor
4 "Hey . . . over here!"
5 Oddsmaker's figure
6 Del Fuego start
7 Hairpieces, informally
8 Columbus campus initials
9 They're worse than mere traffic jams
10 Pub missile
11 Thus, in Latin I
12 Lou Gehrig's number
13 Musical Ma
19 Cumulus lead-in
21 Subdues (with "down")
24 "Against All ___"
25 Bum chaser?
26 Bearing a burden
27 Big name in home video games

Puzzle 40 by Fran & Lou Sabin

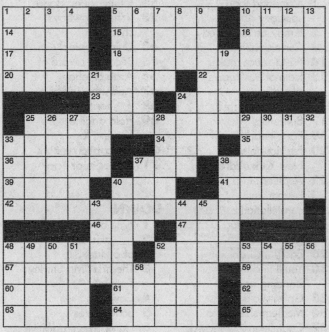

28 Beatles' Eleanor
29 Lower deck
30 He's in the
details, it's said
31 "Mule Train" singer
32 Coastal birds with
wedge-shaped tails
33 Capital of Manche
37 Planet between
Earth and Jupiter
38 French school
40 It's got rhythm
43 Defense org.
since 1949

44 Beauty spot
45 Drops a syllable
48 Rapper-turned-actor
49 Capitol feature
50 Thompson of
"Howards End"
51 Irving and Grant
52 Dry as a ___
53 "Columbo" star
54 Monopoly token
55 Christie's "Death
on the ___"
56 Big blow?
58 Rookery talk

LONG DRIVE

ACROSS

1 Maryland food specialty
5 It may be managed
9 Certain faith
14 Pasta sauce maker
15 Hale of "Gilligan's Island"
16 Buyer be where?
17 Spiderlike
19 Party hearty
20 Fashionable New York address
22 Audition, in a way
23 Palindromic constellation
24 Disney film dog (with "Old")
26 Easily insurable
30 You'll find them standing in malls
33 Golfer Aoki
34 Medium-sized sofa
37 Capt. Jean-___ Picard
38 Machetes originated in the Philippines
40 Parliamentary vote
41 Where some people have it made
43 Pipe joint
44 Early archbishop of Canterbury
47 Words with "sit" or "look"
48 Nielsen or Uggams
50 Type of yard in a Burt Reynolds flick
52 Lake Erie port
55 Japanese drama
56 Ethnic round dance
58 Where cowboys shop?
63 Uninterruptedly
65 Becomes aware of
66 Arab chieftain
67 And others (Abbr.)
68 ___ serif
69 Hold another hearing for
70 Prescribed amount
71 Opposite of ecto-

DOWN

1 Type of casino table
2 ___ avis (one of a kind)
3 The first "Mr. Shirley Temple"
4 Cowboy
5 Solicit votes
6 Hand cream additive
7 Day many save for
8 Endow, as with a quality
9 Mt. Carmel locale
10 Sound investment?
11 Where romantics bowl?
12 Bailiwick
13 Pinochle play
18 Mata ___ (infamous spy)
21 Sommer of film
25 More than fudges
26 Malign in print

Puzzle 41 by Patrick McConville

27 "___ Mio"
28 Where much of the talk is bull?
29 Home and end, for two
31 Acclaim
32 Aroma
35 Golf expendable
36 Like some orders
39 Crossjack, e.g.
42 Certain apartment building
45 At no time, poetically

46 Prop for Mr. Peanut
49 Temporary vehicle
51 Lymph ___
53 Drugged
54 "___ Billie Joe"
56 Earth mover
57 Words with "Lay it" or "The joke's"
59 Memorable periods in world history
60 Infamous czar
61 Blow off steam
62 Classic gas brand
64 Liquor-free

IS THERE A COW IN HERE?

ACROSS

1 Beginning on
5 Three-card scam
10 Almanac entry
14 "Book 'em, ___!" ("Hawaii Five-O" catch phrase)
15 Fencing swords
16 Personal articles case
17 "Happy Days Are Here Again" composer
18 Respond to a stimulus
19 Speck
20 Electronic musical instrument brand
23 Birds that may be spotted
24 Many, many millennia
25 Judicial opinions
28 Fall back, as a tide
31 Plumbers connect them
35 Two ___ kind
36 Tile collage
39 Song for one
40 Rarely
43 Ghost's sound
44 Western or cheese breakfast dish
45 Bean counter, for short
46 Offered one's seat
48 "Do Ya" group, for short
49 Wedding seater
51 Pina colada component
53 Lose star status
55 Othello
63 Dry watercourse

64 Hawaiian island veranda
65 "American ___"
66 Esther, to Lamont Sanford
67 Anatomical cavities
68 Spicy Spanish stew
69 Kill, as a dragon
70 Baltimore football player
71 Jack of Clancy novels

DOWN

1 "___-12" (1968–75 police drama)
2 Starch used as a food thickener
3 "___ Clock Jump" (Basie theme)
4 Couldn't remember
5 Actress Streep
6 Ali Baba's magic words
7 Sans mixers
8 Word with "high" or "Georgia"
9 First name in cosmetics
10 Doctrine that advocates equal rights for women
11 From ___ (the gamut)
12 ___ as a button
13 Wedding cake layer
21 Hindu religious teacher
22 Absorb, as gravy
25 Condemns
26 "___ now, when?"
27 Chocolate bean

Puzzle 42 by Lyle Goddard

29 Biblical tower
30 Restaurant menu
32 Kitty alternative
33 Skip the wedding ceremony
34 Dolphin detector
37 John Lennon's wife
38 Kind of card or ball
41 Immensity
42 Instrumental practice piece
47 Batman and Robin are a "dynamic" one
50 Year on campus

52 Grinding tooth
54 Bird-related
55 "___ the night before Christmas . . ."
56 Transport, as a load
57 Dame Everage
58 Words before "close second" or "fever"
59 "As seen ___" (ad phrase)
60 Sit ___ by (in a lazy manner)
61 Soda selection
62 Zeal

EPIC BATTLE

ACROSS

1 "Light" and "dark" orders
5 Executives' extras
10 Appear
14 "Whip It" band
15 Term of employment
16 Jerry Lewis film "Friend"
17 Jerusalem temple locale
18 Relish
19 Olympian Louganis
20 1876 battle site
23 White flag's message
25 Health resort
26 A shag rug made in Sweden
27 Highly excited (with "up")
28 Marvel Comics heroes and film
32 Red October, for one
34 College credit
36 It's said pitifully
38 Early settlers of Iceland
42 Battle loser Custer
45 Man in a sombrero, perhaps
46 ". . . and ___ the twain shall meet"
47 Kazan of films
48 Word with "little" or "late"
50 Travel by sea
52 Byrnes of "77 Sunset Strip"
53 Sawbones' gp.
56 Have a light repast
58 Batman and Superman have them
60 Battle site, as known today
65 Run easily
66 Part of a Tama or Pearl set
67 "Gone With the Wind" estate
70 Sills solo
71 "Tarzan of the Apes" writer Burroughs
72 Focus group?
73 Shaver's bane
74 There's no accounting for it
75 Invite letters

DOWN

1 Wood-shaping tool
2 Muumuu accessory
3 Controversial theory
4 "Super" Seattle athlete
5 "Want to hear a secret?"
6 Latin catchall citation
7 Split
8 They'll do for openers
9 Peels
10 Lovelorn utterance
11 Trial partner
12 Sort of board
13 ___ cum laude
21 Nickname for a cowboy
22 Thin and bony
23 Goons

Puzzle 43 by Alan Olschwang

24 "Walk Away ___"
    (Four Tops hit)
29 Vivacious actress West
30 Panache
31 Nasal openings
33 Cylinder diameter
35 Race speed, sometimes
37 Small Eurasian duck
39 Acts out
40 Cutting, as a remark
41 Mild expletive
43 Hollywood figure
44 Title in India
49 Beginning

51 Old Sprint rival
53 Part of Poe's signature
54 New Zealand native
55 Meat mold material
57 Zoo attraction,
    perhaps
59 Modify
61 Hard wood
62 Pesters
63 Another mild expletive
64 Where you are
    on a map
68 Gun the engine
69 Cleo's killer

JOINT ACTION

ACROSS

1 "___ / Tuck"
4 Thespian's trophy
9 Type of position
14 Suffix with "hero"
15 Stuff in the attic?
16 Word with zinc or nitrous
17 It may be pulled or bent
18 Cockney's challenge
19 Jewish calendar month
20 Bumbling ones
23 Close again, as an envelope
24 Gray's area?
28 City south of Moscow or pitcher Hershiser
29 Downright unpleasant
32 Prefix for "term" or "wife"
33 Movie critic Roger
35 Flower holders
37 Pasta choice
41 "Meet the ___"
42 Metric measures
43 "I love" to Latin lovers
44 She vanted to be left alone
46 Freelancer's enc.
50 Endangered Florida creature
53 Motion of the ocean result
55 Hilarious
58 So old that it's new
61 Stringed Renaissance instruments

62 Actress Gretchen
63 "The Hollow Men" poet
64 Escape detection
65 Miner's discovery
66 "Divine Poems" author
67 Scotch partners?
68 Chocolate factory need

DOWN

1 Pitching brothers Joe and Phil
2 More mindless
3 Examine closely
4 Bay of Japan
5 Not yet used
6 ___ d'Azur
7 Gothic doorway shape
8 Prepare leftovers
9 "The Grapes of Wrath" actor
10 Occupy time and space
11 "___ better to have loved . . ."
12 This org. has a lot of pull
13 Pro Football Hall of Famer Dawson
21 Famous folks
22 "___ other questions?"
25 Writing on the wall, e.g.
26 "The Drew Carey Show" character
27 PGA measurements
30 Kind of wrestling
31 Garden support

Puzzle 44 by Elizabeth C. Gorski

34 Derek and Jackson
35 BO sign
36 50-50 chance
37 "A Wit's End" author Bombeck
38 Former heavyweight champion Spinks
39 Op. ___ (footnote abbr.)
40 Star of a classic sitcom
41 Grier or Shriver
44 "Wow!" to Beaver Cleaver
45 Passes a rope through

47 "The Gods Themselves" author Isaac
48 Lady in Spain
49 Aerie newborn
51 Ohio's rubber city
52 Gov't security
54 Cathedral parts
56 Minuteman's home?
57 With the volume on 10
58 Roulette play
59 "Turn to Stone" rockers
60 Oz woodman's composition

MAKE SPACE

ACROSS

1 They're withdrawn from
5 Exasperated
10 Risked a few points?
14 Carla portrayer on "Cheers"
15 Yonder
16 Ballerina's move
17 Revenuer's quarry
19 Highly collectible
20 Certain operators
21 Gave one's two cents
23 ". . . lamp ___ my feet"
24 Rock composed of quartz
25 Without alteration
27 It's a wrap!
29 Thomas Lincoln, to family
32 Landscaping tool
34 Dietary, in advertisements
35 Valuable club?
36 "Lethal Weapon 4" actress Russo
37 Avoid, as capture
39 Bed with bars
40 Chang's twin
41 "Pardon me"
42 Sci-fi creatures
44 Sidekick
45 "Evita" role
47 Jazz singer Anita
48 Determine if it's gold

50 Perched on
52 Billboard item
54 First showing
58 "And another thing . . ."
59 Overly romantic
61 Stadium level
62 "Rubber capital of the world"
63 Rugged rock
64 It may go to blazes
65 Theater chain
66 Hard to pin down

DOWN

1 "A Farewell To ___"
2 "O Brother, Where Art ___?"
3 "Is it just ___ is it cold in here?"
4 Optimisticly cheerful
5 "Some Like ___"
6 Horned africans
7 Some collectible dolls
8 Poet's preposition
9 Lowered in rank
10 Sail-crossing spar
11 Solar system models
12 Dublin's land
13 Exploit
18 Common thing
22 Glazier's unit

Puzzle 45 by George Keller

24 Dry as desert sand
25 Where sports events may be held
26 Shades
28 Bowie's last stand
30 Sourish
31 Ball girls
32 Medical ritual, briefly
33 Wedding run-through
38 Exceedingly
39 Flap on medieval breeches

41 Church projection
43 Capacious
46 Taper gradually
49 Macy's, for one
51 Black-capped gulls
52 It's often beaten
53 A little of this, a little of that
54 Trim away
55 "Jane ___"
56 Tangible
57 Showing strain
60 Ref's ring call, sometimes

BODY DOUBLE

ACROSS

1 ___ diem (seize the day)
6 Winged stinger
10 English lord's address
14 Diary publisher Nin
15 Winged
16 Itching to go
17 In-person, as a discussion
19 Astronaut's juice
20 Nationality suffix
21 Park and Madison (Abbr.)
22 Spirited
24 Supply the reception
26 Cat or engine sound
27 One who gets the point?
29 One way to stroll
33 Stretched to the limits
34 Conservative Brits
36 Sputter and stall
37 Storytime meanies
39 End of Rick's toast
40 Action movie highlight
42 Matter for the courts
43 Distinct stages
46 Choice word?
47 One way to see?
49 In demand
51 Eventful times in history
52 "The Luck of Roaring Camp" writer
53 "Swan Lake," e.g.
56 Unvaried
57 "___ Bravo"
60 Decorative window shape
61 How honeymooners may walk
64 ___ the wiser
65 Southernmost Great Lake
66 Elroy Jetson's pet
67 Basin pitcher
68 Prison terms
69 It may have a brand name

DOWN

1 Tearoom relative
2 Collections of anecdotes
3 Pimlico, e.g.
4 It's slapstick material
5 Elvis' Graceland, e.g.
6 Communion host, e.g.
7 "Bummer!"
8 Pouchlike structure
9 Take for granted
10 Second-largest planet
11 "Ghostbusters" director Reitman
12 Word with "ice" or "roller"
13 Impatient and anxious
18 Conspicuous
23 Puritanical person
25 Johnson of "Laugh-In"
26 Company of lions
27 Salt away
28 Shrewd

Puzzle 46 by Gayle Dean

29 Bid the bed adieu
30 Contaminate
31 Certain wash cycle
32 Apportioned (with "out")
35 Sanctions
38 Plant reproductive body
41 Revival site, sometimes
44 Actress Locklear
45 Honored Hindu
48 Employee with lots of money
50 Figure skater's venues
52 Mythological underworld
53 Something to pick?
54 Acknowledge frankly
55 Daily Planet employee
56 Make short cuts?
58 About, formally speaking
59 Something fishy?
62 Palindromic constellation
63 Hawaiian hrs.

BUSY, BUSY, BUSY

ACROSS

1 Herringlike fish
5 Hebrew fathers
10 Org. asking "Where's the beef?"
14 Neck of the woods
15 Kind of coffee or stew
16 World Cup objective
17 Functions perfectly
20 Thread holder
21 Animal restrainer
22 Fairy tale veggie
23 "For Whom the Bell ___"
25 Spanish aunt
27 Beefsteak or cherry
30 "Who Shot J.R.?" show
33 Israeli-designed weapon
34 Addition to the staff?
37 Mischievous pranks
39 Where one's nose may be
43 "Wait ___ Dark" (Hepburn film)
44 Fair to middling
45 "The ___ and the Pendulum"
46 Type of pie
48 Hasty drawing
51 Prefix meaning "outer"
52 "A League of ___ Own" (1992)
54 "Long ___, in a galaxy far . . ."
57 Opening words, for short
59 What a password allows
63 Waste one's breath

66 Natural emollient
67 Start of a famous Schwarzenegger quote
68 Contemporary of Ellery and Agatha
69 Word before "do-well"
70 Carrie portrayer, in film
71 Divination practitioner

DOWN

1 Circular and crosscut
2 Jockey's persuader
3 Prefix with "space"
4 Word in two states' names
5 Require nursing
6 Edible European flatfish
7 Common campus transportation
8 On the Atlantic Ocean
9 California volcano
10 Exclamation of disgust
11 "General Hospital," e.g.
12 Throw down the gauntlet
13 ___ mater
18 One-armed bandit
19 Type of play
24 "___ time no see"
26 Settled onto a branch
27 "Swan Lake" costume
28 Layer with a hole
29 Little League equipment
30 Bear necessities?
31 Sure way to motherhood

Puzzle 47 by Ron Halverson

32 Word with "barrier" or "boom"
35 Approximately
36 Acapulco uncle
38 One of Adam's sons
40 Scout outing
41 Healing potion
42 Reality unit?
47 Calendar pages
49 Chicken ___
50 Kovacs and Pyle
52 Lover's keepsake, perhaps

53 Does owl impressions
54 "Shane" star Ladd
55 Apt family name in "The Wizard of Oz"
56 Orchestra pitch-setter
58 Restaurant choice
60 Ran like heck
61 "Everybody Wants to ___ the World"
62 River through Belgium
64 "Star-Spangled Banner" preposition
65 Chesapeake, e.g.

NICE STARTS

ACROSS

1 Mixologist's measure
5 Judges' attire
10 Young oyster
14 Hawaiian bubbly?
15 Third rock from the sun
16 Grass skirt dance
17 Like some vaccines
18 Sports center
19 Gossip column squib
20 Newcomer's visitor
23 Mars hue
24 Offer a new construction estimate
28 Balloon filler
32 Liner's cheap section
35 Shrine to remember
36 Political coalition
37 Dear Abby's twin
38 What Ed Sullivan specialized in making
42 "___ Gotta Be Me"
43 NASCAR word
44 Artist Matisse or Rousseau
45 Metal craftsman
48 Hindus' holy river
49 Al Capp's Hawkins
50 "Peter ___" (Disney film)
51 Bit of happy mail
59 Stylish elegance
62 Took a chance
63 Niagara noise
64 Black tie affair
65 Kind of period
66 Aware
67 Gem mined in Australia
68 Gantry or Fudd
69 Chick sound

DOWN

1 "___ Dancing" (Johnny Rivers song)
2 Hound's prey
3 Shape of the old pigskin
4 It's lowest on the Mohs scale
5 Hole maker
6 Propelled a wherry
7 Witch's concoction
8 Europe's highest volcano
9 Type of carpet
10 Black eye
11 "___ up or shut up!"
12 Tankard contents
13 Cap with a pompon
21 Celestial hunter
22 Smelter fodder
25 Activity that make keep a shepherd awake
26 Deliberately not notice
27 Funny Menace
28 Convent closetful
29 Ms. Newton-John

Puzzle 48 by Diane C. Baldwin

30 Last or final part of something
31 Start of Cain's query
32 Slow-moving critter
33 Heading for an important list
34 Former French coin
36 Champagne description
39 ___ chi (martial art)
40 Michael of tennis
41 Sawbuck
46 Indicate silently
47 French sea
48 Male goose
50 Musical composition
52 Defeat by a hair
53 Jimmy Carter's middle name
54 Sussex streetcar
55 Riding whip
56 Good rating for steak?
57 Have status
58 Liquid unit
59 Teamwork deterrent
60 Two pool lengths
61 Menu words

DECORATOR'S CHOICE

ACROSS

1 Hoglike rhino relative
6 Well-ventilated
10 Four in a music group
14 Become hardened to
15 DeWitt Clinton's canal
16 Spot for Columbus
17 The remote is pointed a bit higher than this
20 "The ___ and the Pussycat" (lullaby)
21 Greek arrow-shooter
22 Asian peninsula
23 Ditch
25 Homer's dad
27 Some are personal
28 Groups of twenty
30 Black flies, e.g.
32 Astral flareup
33 It catches what a bib cannot
37 Signs, to the superstitious
39 "___ That Jazz" (1979)
40 Painter de Toulouse-Lautrec or Matisse
41 It has four legs
43 Shortly, to Hamlet
44 Plotter's line, perhaps
45 Brawny
47 Exec's degree, perhaps
50 Asian holiday
51 Merry-go-round figure, to a child
52 Suspect's explanation
54 Stereo
55 Oohs' partners
58 Aspirin holder

62 Borscht ingredient
63 Unwanted drip
64 West African capital
65 Church wing
66 Track circuits
67 Smelling a rat

DOWN

1 One of Michael's Jackson's brothers
2 Restart from the beginning
3 Stops, as a speeder
4 Blood pressure raiser
5 "The British are coming" shouter
6 "The Tortoise and the Hare" writer
7 The eyes have it
8 "Blame It on ___" (Caine comedy)
9 Hankering
10 "The Wizard of Oz" dog
11 "Batman" police chief
12 Suffered from homesickness
13 Orders to a jerk?
18 Funds for the golden yrs.
19 Charcoal drawing, e.g.
24 Irritable
25 It's measured in degrees
26 "A Christmas Carol" cry
28 The "white" of "White Christmas"

Puzzle 49 by Lynn Lempel

29 "Catch a Falling Star" crooner Perry

30 Fish organs

31 Fleeces

33 Behavioral pattern

34 Pain in the neck

35 Golfer's choice

36 Tinkle in a phone booth?

38 It might make your hair stand on end

42 Log splitter

45 Where you might rest easy

46 "Survivor" council

47 Poisonous snake

48 Four-letter-word eliminator

49 Helpers

51 Folks from the boonies

53 A mouthful of food

54 Junker of a car

56 German gentleman

57 Spend the night

59 Ailing

60 Teachers' org.

61 What a game may break

HOME RUN

ACROSS

1 He loved his Irish Rose
5 D.C. railway
10 Oliver Twist's request
14 Tailless domestic cat
15 Par ___ (airmail label)
16 Polish writing
17 Doing kitchen duty, to a GI
18 Peter of "M"
19 "Finished!"
20 HOME
23 Used cars
24 First name in "The Ten Commandments" cast
25 In conclusion
28 Hammer-wielding god
30 Hair goop, e.g.
33 Snow White and the seven dwarfs, collectively
34 Thick partner
35 Burger and fries go-with
36 HOME
39 Spike and Ang
40 Foreign currency
41 A delivery person may have one
42 Fashion monogram
43 Formally surrender
44 Evening star
45 Stomach muscles
46 Seemingly forever
47 HOME
54 Off one's rocker
55 Address the crowd
56 Butterfingers' exclamation
57 Privy to
58 Princeton mascot
59 Atlas datum
60 Daly of "Judging Amy"
61 Crystal ball gazers
62 Cervine creature

DOWN

1 Crazed way to run
2 Source of misery
3 Like cuttlefish defenses
4 They send goods abroad
5 Chronic ailment
6 Conjure up
7 It keeps on rolling
8 Calhoun of Westerns
9 Single file
10 It may be worn on the chest
11 Something sensed
12 Produce protection
13 Summer in Paris
21 "Cape Fear" star
22 Word in a Thornton Wilder play title
25 Humble in position
26 Charley horses, e.g.
27 "___ Magnolias"
28 Limerick starter
29 Start of a Sleepy refrain?
30 Rose

Puzzle 50 by Mark Milhet

31 The best and
   the brightest
32 Kind of printer
34 Sound of a
   none-too-gentle
   landing
35 One paved surface
   across another, e.g.
37 Certain drives
38 Sports complex
43 TV network
   up north
44 Electorate
45 Right things?

46 Aromatic organic
   compound
47 Small equine
48 Computer command
   symbol
49 One of the
   Great Lakes
50 Over-the-top anger
51 Excessive
   bloodshed
52 Dueling weapon
53 Overlord of old
54 Three sheets
   to the wind

MAKE IT SNAPPY!

ACROSS

1 Big name in aluminum
6 Newts in transition
10 "___ Was a Rollin' Stone" (1972 hit)
14 "Absolutely not!"
15 Playwright Coward
16 It's south of the Caspian
17 Get a move on
19 Dollar portion
20 Compass point
21 Bits of reality?
22 Get by on thin ice?
23 In great part
26 Commandment starter
28 Homophone of you
29 Falls in Wisconsin
33 Supplement
36 Nut case
37 Word with "dash" or "stick"
38 Move a bit faster
41 Software purchaser
42 Items driven off of
43 Voice above baritone
44 Realized
46 Pool stick
47 Chesapeake Bay creature
48 Nighttime visitor of folklore
52 Kind of signal
55 They cross the charts
57 Santa ___, Calif.
58 TV vehicle for Judd Hirsch
59 Hightail it

62 Film featuring Damien (with "The")
63 One of the back forty
64 Hold in high esteem
65 Hunger message
66 ___ moss
67 Winner in a famous 1948 headline

DOWN

1 Wilderness photographer Adams
2 "___ luck!"
3 "Give me an A . . . ," e.g.
4 Alley ___ (pass and dunk)
5 Hole-punching gadget
6 Notch below ambassador
7 Opponents
8 Events with Jerry Lewis
9 Cunning
10 Accelerate
11 Wilderness or staging, e.g.
12 Cool off like a boxer
13 Poker fee
18 Twiddling one's thumbs
22 Soak up gravy
24 Hop to it
25 "Return of the Jedi" furball
27 Boot camp outing
29 Spoke lovingly
30 Liveliness

Puzzle 51 by James E. Buell

31 Home of Baylor University
32 Copycat
33 Blue tinged with green
34 It's something to sneeze at
35 Practice girth control
36 Certain joint support
39 Volcano near Messina
40 Knock for a loop
45 Wrath
46 Curtain call lineup
48 Like Georgia Brown
49 Showy parrot

50 Body part that may sometimes be "twisted"
51 Thoroughly unpleasant
52 What to do "in the name of love"
53 Angie Dickinson role
54 Large bovine
56 Pod vegetable
59 Where X marks the spot
60 Color that "suits" Santa
61 Hatchet relative

IN SHAPE

ACROSS

1 "To ___, With Love" (1967)
4 Removes from a manuscript
9 Relinquish, as an office
14 "Detective" portrayed by Jim Carrey
15 Send to seventh heaven
16 Words with "hole" or "two"
17 Batten down the hatches
20 Perceive sound
21 Copyright symbol
22 In the middle of
23 Former CNN correspondent Peter
25 Synthetic fabric
27 Words of approximation
29 Set on edge
33 Hot Tex-Mex dish
36 Became discolored
38 Parliamentary vote
39 It's between Daniel and Joel
40 Actress Zadora
41 Watering hole items
43 Boxing legend from Kentucky
44 Wynonna's mom
46 Analyze ore
47 Decorative patterns
49 Diplomat's forte
51 Jingles
53 Quickie portrait
57 Antique dealer's transaction, e.g.
60 Take on a role
62 Perry's creator
63 Has some French toast?
66 Leaflike plant part
67 Brilliant achievement
68 "___ we having fun yet?"
69 Seaweed and kelp, e.g.
70 Wooded valleys
71 "___ Little Indians"

DOWN

1 "Borat" portrayer ___ Baron Cohen
2 More likely to cause a winter skid
3 Aired "The Brady Bunch," today
4 Marina ___ Rey
5 Votes into office
6 "Better ___ than never"
7 Old operating room substance
8 "What did I tell you?"
9 Certain rattlesnake or terrapin
10 Detroit pistons are found here?
11 Type of ring that goes with bell-bottoms
12 Bed-and-breakfasts
13 Classroom event
18 It's spoken in Louisiana and Haiti
19 "True Grit" star
24 Measure using trigonometry
26 Like some coffee orders
28 Be against

Puzzle 52 by Ron Halverson

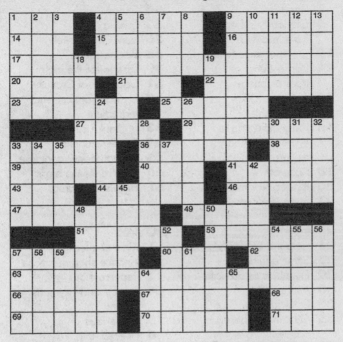

30 Some bakery loaves
31 Mel's Diner waitress
32 Street for the wealthy?
33 Everett of "Medical Center"
34 Target on the golf course
35 Goddess of fertility
37 "Ready, ___, fire!"
42 Admiration
45 Sexton and Bancroft
48 Source of the Mississippi
50 Body that's heavenly

52 Spaghetti topper
54 Halloween option
55 ___ Boothe Luce
56 Her face "launched a thousand ships"
57 McEntire of Nashville
58 British nobleman
59 Party animal?
61 Telephone
64 Abbreviation in a proof
65 They're certainly not from around here

YOU SNOOZE YOU LOSE

ACROSS

1 Hoax
5 Obviously suffering from insomnia
10 ___ spumante (wine)
14 Dense clump of trees or bushes
15 A Gotham City crime-fighter
16 Long-lasting do
17 Word with "fine" or "graphic"
18 Doze off
20 It's slapstick material
21 Soda jerk's creation
22 Elevates
23 Intrude
25 Help the economy
27 Some equines
29 Exemplar of strength
30 Mini end?
33 Editorial view
35 Certain raspberry pastry
37 The former French Sudan
38 Get a good night's sleep
41 Somewhat painful
42 Norse god of discord
43 High points of a South American trip?
44 Matter for the courts
45 "8 Heads in a Duffel ___" 1997
46 "Angela's ___: A Memoir" (Frank McCourt)

48 Aussie pals
50 Snooze
53 Lend a hand
56 Venetian farewell
58 Bovine sound
59 Turn in for the night
61 Daughter of Cronus
62 Lip balm or cosmetics ingredient
63 Sri Lanka currency
64 Former student
65 Acknowledges applause
66 They're for the birds
67 High school areas

DOWN

1 Kind of infection
2 Antique shop purchase
3 Repercussions
4 Everest and Olympus, briefly
5 Mysterious
6 Fleeced item
7 Lies adjacent
8 They're all in the family
9 Prayer
10 Lacewing's snack
11 Homophone for seize
12 Lemur's hangout
13 Dennis the Menace types
19 Lost buoyancy
21 Glee
24 Skater Kerrigan
26 "The Merchant of Venice" heroine
28 Larry or Moe

Puzzle 53 by Gayle Dean

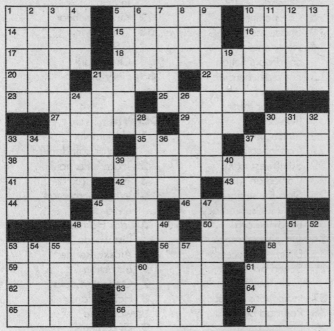

30 "Beautiful" way
to be paid?
31 Actress Sommer
32 Errant shot
33 Mark of Zorro?
34 "Arsenic and Old ___"
36 Old Testament vessel
37 Searched for
gold, in a way
39 Gives out compliments
40 Marine game fish
45 Uptown shindig
47 Reptiles that are
the hair of Medusa

48 Tiny arachnids
49 It can be attached
to "land" or "sea"
51 A funny thing
happened on
the way here
52 ___ at the mouth
(becomes angry)
53 Moby Dick pursuer
54 Missile housing
55 Stevedores do it
57 Frosted
60 Be litigious
61 Witch, to Shakespeare

PRACTICE YOUR VOWELS

ACROSS

1 "Buenos ___!"
5 Competent
10 Shapeless mass
14 First name in courtroom fiction
15 Euripides heroine
16 Fall short
17 Relief for thirsty livestock
20 Button, to Frosty
21 Capitol call
22 Southwest sights
23 Comedian Mort
25 Stats for sluggers
27 Fight for supremacy
31 Lobbying org.
34 Turnpike entrance
35 D.D.E. predecessor
36 Speed away (with "out")
37 Indications of decay
38 Railroad beam
39 Newspapers, Radio and TV
40 Mt. Olympus ruler
41 Miniscule
42 Unhappiness
43 Guinness Book suffix
44 Not entirely joking
46 Got ripped
47 Enjoys a loopy craft
48 Identity disguiser
51 By way of
53 Suffix for suffering body parts
56 Picnicker's worry
60 Classic cookie
61 He was Santa in "Elf"
62 Kind of school
63 "The Crying ___" (1992)
64 Cluttered
65 Fiery Sicilian

DOWN

1 "Mountain ___" (film or soft drink)
2 Today's Persia
3 Type of sax
4 What a crowned head does?
5 Jack Horner's last words
6 Alaska Range attraction
7 On tenterhooks
8 Hall of Fame wannabe
9 Pit contents, perhaps
10 Type of music
11 Fireplace supply
12 Fed. workplace monitor
13 Harry's wife
18 Monarchs' holdings
19 Leave unacknowledged
24 Like a cool cat
26 Word of exception
27 Firewater
28 High points of a South American trip?

Puzzle 54 by Lynn Lempel

29 Speckled swimmer
30 Recipient of a stop order?
31 "Don Quixote" role
32 Theme of this puzzle, or practice writing your vowels, really
33 Hammer features
36 View enhancer
38 Air
39 Like some enemies
41 General assembly?
42 Land's end
44 Place for a run

45 Phases
46 Lake near Carson City
48 Enthralled
49 Pasternak heroine
50 Two stars dating, e.g.
52 Hostelries
54 "The Big Chill" star, William
55 Genesis garden
57 Zodiac creature
58 "Eureka!" for one
59 Whirlpool

DINNER AND A MOVIE

ACROSS

1 Machine opening
5 Word with "tag" or "double"
9 Healer on the Enterprise
14 Melon, cucumbers, pumpkin, etc.
15 Nasty brute
16 ___ and kicking
17 Throaty cousin of "psst!"
18 Notify of risk
19 Little bits
20 Archaeologist's measuring technique
23 Do a chore at the blackboard
24 Delhi streetwear
25 Tape deck button
28 Salver
31 Took by the hand
32 Santa ___
33 Voluminous do
36 Eve follower
38 ". . . Peter, pumpkin ___"
40 Risking one's neck
43 Legal aid
44 ___ noire
45 Some are tops
46 Spot in the mer
47 Seamy matter?
49 ___ of mind
51 Mass. hrs.
52 Brewer's tubs
54 Football variety
58 Visual aid
61 Wing it
64 American food staple
65 Fish organ
66 Belief
67 Like the Gobi
68 Arachnid-appropriate prefix
69 English county
70 Tennis dividers
71 Simmer

DOWN

1 Maneuvering room
2 "The Merry Widow" composer
3 "Carmen" or "Norma"
4 O.K. Corral locale
5 Word with "ghost" or "boom"
6 "Oh my!"
7 It spelled curtains for Polonius
8 Imaginary string around the finger
9 Theme
10 Sabot
11 Op ___
12 Lab eggs
13 No negator
21 Atop, in poesy
22 Dander
25 Two-to-one, e.g.
26 Kind of territory

27 Pasta, potatoes and the like, briefly
29 Latin 101 word
30 "No sweat!"
33 Playing marble
34 Young zebras
35 Hardware for Rosie
37 Map abbreviation
39 Many superheroes have them
41 Dash cache
42 Teacher's org.
48 Funny Charlotte

50 Two cents worth
53 Midnight rumble
55 Public decree
56 "Cape Fear" actor
57 Visibly happy
58 Pro or con
59 Coarse particles
60 Word with "front" or "rear"
61 Impeccable service
62 ER workers
63 Guitarist Paul

LAND-HO!

ACROSS

1 Leg, in slang
4 Speculators' concerns
9 "In Like ___," (1967 Coburn film)
14 Hi, in Spain
15 Moral code
16 Beverly Hills Drive
17 Astronaut's "fine"
18 Land depletion cause, maybe
20 "___ Boots Are Made for Walkin'"
22 Cornmeal breads
23 Actor Jackson of "Pulp Fiction"
25 Like a straphanger
30 Unjustified
32 Sincerely flatter?
33 G-men and T-men
35 Doctor in a 1964 movie
37 Trial companion
38 Luxury site?
39 Street gang combat
42 Grenade ingredient
43 Heep of fiction
45 Tina of "30 Rock"
46 TV's "___-Team"
47 Melancholy poems
50 Obscure
52 Like a ghost town
54 Married woman, in Madrid
57 Makeshift money
59 Road machine
60 Slides into a base

65 "All About ___" (1950 Bette Davis movie)
66 Sporting wings
67 Beethoven's last symphony
68 "Midnight ___" (1988)
69 Frank Wright's middle name
70 Suffix for "usher"
71 Breeze source

DOWN

1 Billy, Nanny and the kids?
2 Hawaiian greeting
3 What kids may do after the rain
4 Tend to the bird feeder
5 Figure skater Midori
6 "Old Ironsides," for one
7 Some metric weights
8 Start of an act
9 Less genial
10 ___ Gatos, California
11 Forest Whitaker's Oscar role
12 "The Matrix" hero
13 Proverbial brickload
19 Squeeze an orange
21 Phoenix five
24 "To Sir, With Love" singer
26 8 1/2"×11" size (Abbr.)

Puzzle 56 by Jim Page

27 Bulldozers
28 "JFK" director Oliver
29 Simmons rival
31 Something to
   bend on a human
33 Like chimneys
34 Country's Steve
36 Part of OTB
39 Craved
40 "Charlotte's ___"
   (1973)
41 Approving votes
44 Survey blank
46 Frank's daughter

48 ___ A Sketch
49 Calm and unruffled
51 Plumb line measures
53 "I ___ my way . . ."
   (Sinatra)
55 Nightclub production
56 Tampa Bay's
   Ice Palace
58 Four gills
60 Actor Holbrook
61 Conceived leader?
62 Chinese way
63 Oink-filled pen?
64 Road map abbr.

GET SOME EXERCISE

ACROSS

1 "Look ___, I'm Sandra Dee"
5 Beet variety
10 Nasty shock
14 Study all night
15 "The Simpsons" dad
16 Youngstown's state
17 Performs a certain exercise
20 Parting remark
21 Kind of wave
22 "Say what?"
23 Metric work unit
25 Snug bug's place
27 Glances at briefly
36 Trial judge Lance
37 Type of blockade
38 Inscribed pillar
39 Naldi of the Ziegfeld Follies
41 They represent trillions
43 Nutmeg coat
44 "Mars Attacks!" genre
46 Designated PG-13
48 "___ had so many children . . ."
49 Grieve inconsolably
52 Expunge
53 Oilcan letters
54 "___ to a Nightingale"
57 Insinuate
61 State known for its potatoes
65 Renounce interest in
68 Biblical twin
69 More frost-covered

70 Small accessory case
71 Adjust with a wedge
72 "USA, USA, USA," for one
73 Kind of board in a pub

DOWN

1 ___ fool (goof off)
2 Stepped heavily
3 A Hawaiian island
4 Masters of ceremonies
5 Bearded revolutionary
6 Party thrower
7 Mine, in Marseilles
8 Tear apart
9 Bleak
10 Write hastily
11 "Here comes trouble!"
12 In ___ of (instead of)
13 Reggae artist Peter
18 Second largest of the Great Lakes
19 Twists around
24 No-see-um, e.g.
26 Jim Croce's "I ___ Name"
27 Dishwasher cycle
28 New York thruway city
29 Tag game call
30 "Miss ___ Boys" (1997)
31 "The Divine" Vaughan

32 Send to seventh heaven

33 Left-hand page

34 Nobel Peace Prize winner Root

35 Rent to another tenant

40 Get an ___ effort

42 Baltic and Adriatic

45 Architect Jones

47 Things go down it

50 Like paradise

51 Spread hay

54 Has bills

55 Hyphen's cousin

56 Actor Morales

58 Kind of support

59 Pacific Rim region

60 ". . . and ___ some"

62 Charles' family pet, in film

63 "Rush ___" (Jackie Chan/Chris Tucker movie)

64 "Think nothing ___"

66 Engine sound you love to hear

67 Gallery display

CAPITAL IDEA!

ACROSS

1 Pieces of two-pieces
5 Small progression
9 Addis ___ (Ethiopia's capital)
14 Tube diameter
15 "Last Action ___" (1993)
16 Docket fill
17 Actress Blanchett
18 Complain, complain, complain
19 Pleasant surprise
20 It's a capital place
23 Bradley and Trixie's husband
24 Comstock load
25 Brings to the boiling point
29 Wet, spongy ground
31 Some are natural, some are broken
35 Takes wing
36 Object in a quiver
38 Child seat?
39 It's a capital place
42 Palindromic conjunction
43 ". . . ___ evil, speak . . ."
44 Audio signal receiver
45 Put through the paces
47 Word with "takers" or "day now"
48 Takes the helm
49 They precede mis, on a music scale
51 Haggard work
52 It's a capital place
60 18 holes, for example
61 "Honeybunch"
62 They may be beaten
64 Compel through coercion
65 No one's in until this is put in
66 Got on one's high horse?
67 Trusty mount
68 Unpleasant situation
69 Otherwise

DOWN

1 "I, Claudius" network
2 "The Long and Winding ___"
3 "Laugh-In" comedian Johnson
4 "As ___ on TV!"
5 Does an office chore
6 They're shed
7 Roberts of "Runaway Train"
8 Game of chukkers
9 Action may make him laugh or cry?
10 Wine container
11 On the Baltic
12 Form droplets
13 Regarding
21 Lawsuit preposition
22 Get ready to surf
25 Coveted quality
26 Dame's introduction?
27 Stares with open mouth

Puzzle 58 by George Keller

28 Newsworthy period of history
29 Like the ocean
30 Yes ___ (one of two answers)
32 Not with another
33 Spring offering
34 Practices for a boxing match
36 Communicant's word
37 Damper
40 The absolute minimum
41 Cash's boy, in a song
46 Hypnotic sleep
48 Coastlines
50 Finished
51 Part of a full house?
52 Canine sounds
53 Horn sound
54 Work as a barker
55 Father of Cain and Abel
56 Tunney of the ring
57 Horror film fare
58 Adored one
59 Increases (with "to")
63 Figure out

EMOTIONS IN MOTION

ACROSS

1 Routine auto maintenance job
5 Improvise, musically
9 Graphic symbols
14 Predatory shorebird
15 Magnetic recording medium
16 Two make a diameter
17 Shoulder muscle, for short
18 Muscle malady
19 Use a pew for support
20 Person that's pointed at
23 Thing in a court document
25 Like the fabled piper
26 "60 Minutes" personality
27 Beaver State
29 Crater mouths
30 Real pity
33 Graceful dance step
36 Intellectually acute
37 "At Seventeen" singer Janis
38 Arctic floater
39 Fabric measures, briefly
40 Old-fashioned introduction
44 Mouth off
45 Immature egg
46 Pressing
49 Movie pooch
51 It may pave the way
52 Cause of a scene, perhaps
55 Dressing choice
56 Type of cost
57 Hand lender
60 Lawn maintenance tool
61 Proofreader's notation, perhaps
62 Nice and cozy
63 Bassoon accessories
64 Some ladies of the field
65 Ebullient

DOWN

1 Trip instigator
2 Four-stringed instrument
3 Things to shoot for
4 "I could ___ horse!"
5 Putting on, as a theatrical production
6 Secret stash
7 Pest for a rose
8 Parent's challenge, sometimes
9 Aggravating
10 Choral music parts
11 Start of a Keats title
12 Sister's kid
13 Smooth and lustrous
21 Versed in
22 Pretty hopeless
23 "Gonna Fly Now" flick
24 Goofed up

Puzzle 59 by Diane C. Baldwin

28 Singapore sling ingredient
29 Indian royalty
31 River sediment
32 Cinematic mainframe
33 Child's toy
34 Heart outlet
35 Memorial meal
38 TV-regulating Agency
40 Some gaits
41 Hostile to
42 Takes minutes
43 Capricorn's symbol

44 Practiced conservation
46 One who may put you in your place
47 ___ Island Red (chicken)
48 Chisel mark
49 Former Veep Spiro
50 Happy face feature
53 Stocking shade
54 Place for la familia
58 Batman and Robin, e.g.
59 Word with "timer" or "roll"

GOLDIE OLDIES

ACROSS

1 Huey Lewis & the News tune "I Want ___ Drug"
5 Hanging tapestry with pictorial designs
10 What a crow's-nest is attached to
14 Adam and Eve's youngest son to be mentioned in the Bible
15 Bobby Knight, for one
16 Soothing plant extract found in many cosmetics and lotions
17 1970 Jack Lemmon-Sandy Dennis movie
20 Commit a faux pas
21 Break in friendly relations
22 Puts up, as a skyscraper
23 Hosiery mishap
24 Diddley, Jackson and Derek
25 Type of room in cyberspace
26 Tehran is its capital
28 1995 film, "Operation Dumbo ___"
29 Term before "carte" or "mode"
32 The Moody Blues' "Nights in White ___"
34 Offensive facial expression
35 "I Dream of Jeannie" star
36 Goldie Hawn film
39 On the quiet side, nautically
40 Racetrack fence
41 Notched like a maple leaf
42 Maritime distress call
43 It's after penultimate
44 Director of "Collateral"
45 Source of an artist's inspiration
46 "The Bridge of ___ Luis Rey"
47 Kabibble of Kay Kyser's band or suffix meaning "about"
50 Sneak attack
53 Type of splints that are a problem for joggers
54 Disco guy on "The Simpsons"
55 Comedy that included Meryl Streep, Bruce Willis and Isabella Rossellini
58 Perry Mason's creator Gardner
59 Make reparations
60 Tangible, not virtual
61 "___ I say more?"
62 Looked at with open mouth
63 Likelihood ratio

DOWN

1 Daisylike bloom
2 Indira Gandhi's father
3 Endless time periods
4 Doctor of sci-fi
5 Director's shout
6 Gable and mansard
7 White water vehicle
8 Legislation creation
9 Footwear seller's implement
10 "Luncheon on the Grass" painter Edouard
11 One of the Baldwin boys
12 Arrange in a logical order
13 1979 Nastassja Kinski title role
18 University of Illinois locale
19 Call it a day on the set

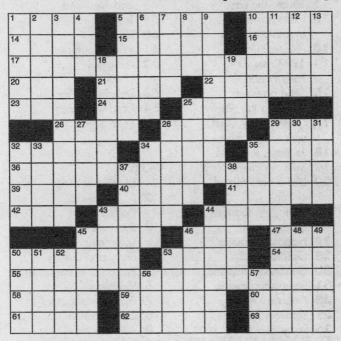

25 Fisherman's wicker basket
27 Tear asunder
28 "Left-handed" accounting entry
29 Chastised
30 Organic necklaces
31 Singer Murray or author Rice
32 Mineral springs
33 "Alice's Restaurant" singer
34 A renter may break it
35 Bring home the bacon
37 Dumpster item
38 Actress Tripplehorn

43 Rife with vegetation
44 Having a part of the body crippled
45 Used the remote to eliminate sound
46 Glistened
48 Word before "fast" and after "home"
49 Flings with force
50 Arabian Sea gulf
51 "A ___ formality"
52 Cotton unit
53 Old English bard
56 LAX posting
57 Letters indicating a sold-out performance

ORDERLY PROGRESSION

ACROSS

1 Situate the car
5 Hall's partner, in music
10 Mountain route
14 1997 role for Peter Fonda
15 Send payment
16 Involving the ear
17 Open pastry filled with fruit or custard
18 January, in Spain
19 Mlle., in Puerto Rico
20 Like a naturalized citizen
23 "Bali ___" (South Pacific song)
24 Nagasaki natives
25 Clairvoyance
30 Geisha's garment
31 Be encumbered to
32 Nabokov novel
35 Throw violently
36 Party to a 1993 peace accord
37 Justifiable
39 Simple resting place
40 My follower, in Vietnam
41 Count (on)
42 Harsh interrogation
45 Clear from accusation
48 Words with "distance" or "glance"
49 Time
56 "Put a sock ___!"
57 Swallows hastily

58 Agnetha, Benny, Bjorn and Anni-Frid
59 Teeter
60 Genesis
61 Wildlife refuge
62 Punta del ___, Uruguay
63 Deteriorates by use
64 Card with three main pips

DOWN

1 Dragon of song
2 "___ Have to Do Is Dream"
3 Service entrance, sometimes
4 Berry and Griffey
5 Pizza sauce enhancer
6 Virgil epic
7 Govt. investigators
8 Cork location
9 Attic function
10 Type of note
11 Skylit courts
12 Withhold release of
13 Glances at
21 Narrow leather strip
22 Vesuvius output
25 Missile housing
26 Give off
27 Kind of artist
28 Neither liquid nor gaseous
29 ___ Jima
30 Place for a bucket of food

Puzzle 61 by George Keller

32 Mariner's direction
33 Wine partner
34 Use an abacus
36 Average score for Tiger
37 Meat avoider
38 Financing factor, initially
40 "3rd Rock from the Sun" star
41 Loathes
42 Sometimes it comes out of its shell

43 Producer's dream
44 Piano pedal
45 Flaming
46 Dairy Queen purchases
47 Librarian's command
50 Frank Herbert novel
51 Ingrid Bergman role
52 Shaken crystals
53 Building beam
54 Award sponsored by the Village Voice
55 Not one, in Dogpatch

OO!

ACROSS
1 Nautical pronouns
5 Scientific information
9 Eucharist offering
14 Converse
15 Turns someone into a patsy
16 Eat at the bank?
17 Pro's foe
18 Excellent, in street talk
19 Cursor targets
20 Pleasing to the eye
23 Bodybuilder's target
24 Start a paragraph
25 Certain restaurant's acronym
27 Legendary Giant slugger
28 Suggestive of an idyll
32 Confuse
35 In need of kneading
36 Chaplin persona
37 "How was ___ know?"
38 Laertes' sister in "Hamlet"
41 "The ramparts" lead-in
42 Bird in a crazy simile
44 It has many body parts
45 Civilian clothes
47 Assigns the care of
49 Pied Piper devotee
50 Rational mentally
51 Vacation destination, perhaps
54 Word with "aside," "down," "out" or "on"

56 It may cause a stir
60 Type of bacteria
62 "___ I say more?"
63 "___ the wild blue yonder"
64 Century plants
65 "Do it or ___!"
66 Gulf bordered by Somalia
67 Wound application
68 Fortuneteller
69 Airplane part

DOWN
1 Prenuptial party
2 '60s war capital
3 "Candle in the Wind" singer John
4 Word after 23, in a phrase
5 Company that discovered nylon
6 "___ in the Dark"
7 Hardwood source
8 Piedmont wine city
9 Dumbbell, e.g.
10 Bow-shaped line
11 Leaving no opportunity for error
12 Ms. Ferber
13 Take a nap
21 Release
22 Japanese-American
26 La la preceder
28 Ruth Lilly Prize winners
29 One of the Guthries
30 Criminally assist

Puzzle 62 by Isaiah Burke

31 Petty or Singer
of the cinema

32 Caustic comments

33 School on the
River Thames

34 Place to rest
one's tootsies

35 Eyelid position

39 Bullfighters' entrance
march

40 Gather, as details

43 Org. with many arms

46 Impracticably ideal

48 Imprudent

49 Melt down, as fat

51 Actress Della

52 Part of a sonata

53 Lugs along

54 Mendel studied them

55 Francis Ford Coppola's
alma mater

57 "The Defiant
___" (1958)

58 Remove print

59 Amount in an
Agatha Christie title

61 "My Name is
Asher ___"

WEIRD MATH

ACROSS

1 Stopped lying?
6 "Little Orphan Annie" character (with "The")
9 Oscar de la ___
14 Type of angle
15 By way of
16 Localities
17 Just my opinion, and then some?
20 "A mouse!"
21 Go downhill
22 Teaspoonful, perhaps
23 Burns of documentaries
24 Canonical hour
26 "Arabian Nights" characters
30 Venerate
34 Bonnie Parker portrayer Dunaway
35 Literature's Papa
38 It's for two, in song
39 Cowboy accessory, and then some
42 Amount of work, according to a busy person
43 Tumultuous
44 Sniggler's haul
45 Pass the bill
47 Law feature
49 Lettuce unit
52 Acoustic organ
53 Toast spread
56 Most knowing

59 Draft choice
62 Stubbly growth, and then some?
65 Bank job
66 Directly, directionally
67 Notched and jagged
68 Daisylike flower
69 O'Neill and Asner
70 Stands

DOWN

1 Fill completely
2 Workout woe
3 Istanbul inhabitant
4 Multipurpose vehicle, briefly
5 TV "Playhouse" star Herman
6 Assert
7 Dastardly deeds
8 Eucharist plate
9 Inflamed
10 Wore away
11 Suicidal emperor
12 Uses a shuttle
13 Legendary name in tennis
18 Nunnery
19 ___-cone (icy confection)
23 Chicken dish
25 Org. celebrating 60 years in 2009
26 Claw

Puzzle 63 by Ron Halverson

27 Serengeti beast
28 Therefore
29 Traffic mess
31 Catchall category
32 England, to Elizabeth II
33 Greasy spoon sign
34 Elaborate party
36 Sailor's saint
37 Trickery
40 Noble Italian name
41 Dear companion?
46 Eliminate alternatives
48 Convene

50 It's punched with
51 Calculator part
53 Grp. concerned with safety
54 Equivocator's forte
55 Escape route
57 Missile type
58 Scratches by (with "out")
59 Chaotic happenings
60 Take a beating
61 Cote members
63 Midpoint (Abbr.)
64 Mr. Onassis

EATING WELL

ACROSS

1 "Forever Your Girl" singer, Paula
6 Entrance into society
11 Toward a ship's tail
14 New Zealand native
15 Upper crust
16 Sine ___ non
17 Mom's cure-all
19 It may be bookmarked
20 Lamarr of "Samson and Delilah"
21 Remembrance of things past
23 Birthplace of Saint Francis
26 Person who digs hard rock?
28 Type of light in the big city
29 Characters in a Tchaikovsky ballet
31 Beatles song "Back in the ___"
35 Street in some horror movies
36 Baby kangaroos
37 Conductor Zubin
38 Meals for fundamentalists?
41 Something acquired at a wedding?
42 Poetic grief
43 Garner
44 Early offspring
45 Famous person, informally
46 Stubborn creature
47 Forest place

49 Act of Contrition reciter
51 Legendary lumberjack
54 Armor plate that protects the chest
55 67.5 degrees, direction-wise
56 Like an easy crossword, to some
62 "Cries and Whispers" star Ullmann
63 Declare legally void
64 Golf course shouts
65 Terminate ungraciously
66 Pieces of lemon peel
67 Drinks from a flask

DOWN

1 Gremlin's creator
2 "___, humbug!"
3 "And how!"
4 Ragamuffin
5 Has a soft spot for
6 One-third of a liar's policy
7 Overhead trains
8 Life story, shortly
9 Complete reversals
10 Conical quarters
11 Marine or plane starter
12 Roll up, as a flag
13 "Long ___ Sally"
18 Inventor with a bright idea
22 Oil container
23 Lacking vitality
24 Jennifer Lopez biopic
25 Iman, at birth

Puzzle 64 by Alice Walker

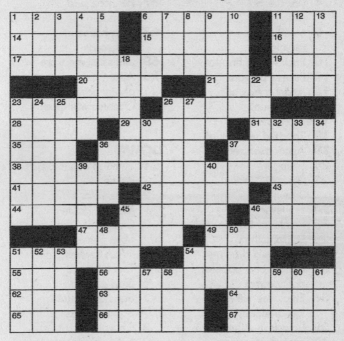

26 Something to
dance around
27 Brogan cushion
30 Type of bliss
32 James Clavell novel
33 TV's Remington
34 Set of horizontal lines
36 Skull part
37 Cause damage to
39 Having a sharp flavor
40 Island united with
Trinidad
45 Eyetooth
46 1980 Olympics site

48 City in western Bolivia
50 Spats
51 Lugosi of "The Raven"
52 Computer operating
system
53 Field of granular snow
54 Snakelike fish
57 Naval off.
58 Director's cry
59 Stepfather of
John F. Kennedy, Jr.
60 It's tapped into
61 Road shape,
sometimes

PPRETTY PPLEASE

ACROSS
1 Decides on (with "for")
5 Metal to be recycled
10 Rock wren's habitat
14 Pirate's plunder
15 Andean republic
16 Holly plant
17 Top-drawer
18 Reached in amount
19 Application request
20 Losing it
23 Grier of "Jackie Brown"
24 However
25 Painter of Olympia
28 Do something
31 Swing era drummer
35 Middle of a popular palindrome
36 Employee with lots of money
39 Vowels in Athens
40 Clamming up
43 Passion
44 Signify
45 Grassy expanse
46 TV dragon
48 Stimpy's buddy
49 Suspicious
51 Tiberius' 1051
53 Kind of symbol
54 Showing and telling
63 Prepare for viewing
64 Abetted
65 Scored the highest grade
66 Moreover
67 Peruvian pack animal
68 Trevi Fountain coin, once
69 Statistical measure
70 Apply, as a phony accent
71 Oceanic whirlpool

DOWN
1 Swedish politician Palme
2 "The Color of Money" game
3 Collette of "The Sixth Sense"
4 Wide treeless plain
5 Theater drop
6 Biggers sleuth
7 Square in Madison Square Garden?
8 Chorale contributor
9 Indiana's state flower
10 Medieval musician
11 Mideast carrier
12 Big rig
13 Gave the boot
21 Singer Page
22 Mouse spotter's cry
25 ___-soprano
26 Disney's Little Mermaid
27 Himalayan kingdom
28 Rags-to-riches figure
29 Exact copy
30 Mortise mate
32 Of some use

Puzzle 65 by George Keller

33 Plate material
34 Analyze a metallic compound
37 "Howards ___" (1992)
38 Abbr. in some military names
41 "Paper Lion" author
42 Palindromic tennis star
47 Pharmaceutical giant ___ Lilly
50 Let it all out
52 Collectively
53 Passenger car
54 Mets, Jets or Nets

55 Waiting around doing nothing
56 Tuscan town on the Arno
57 "Monster" that's really a lizard
58 Anita who sang with 31-Across
59 Skipper of the Nautilus
60 Etching fluid
61 Eggheady sort, stereotypically
62 Big moment in WWII

HELP WANTED

ACROSS

1 Describe in great detail
5 "The Parent ___" (1961)
9 "___ Good Men" (1992)
13 Buck add-on
14 Aquino's successor in the Philippines
16 "To Sir, With Love" singer
17 Ernie's "Sesame Street" pal
18 "It's the end of ___"
19 Tracts of land in the Seine
20 "___ Called Wanda"
22 Kind of triangle
24 Cashew's product
26 Lazy and black-eyed
27 Rodeo equipment
29 Become firm
30 Word omitted in alphabetization
33 Grab, as power
35 "Already?"
37 Bryn ___ College
40 Distressing letters found 8 times in this puzzle
42 Mimicked
43 Barkers' pitches
46 Racetrack site
49 Type of porch
50 "You betcha"
52 Sycophant
55 Boats with paddles
58 Palace of Paris
60 Some Starbucks listings

63 Blender brand
64 Silver-tongued
65 Tablelands
67 Latin word on a dollar bill
68 Awe-struck expression
69 "All the world's a ___"
70 Maglie and Mineo
71 Columnist's page, briefly
72 Mideast gulf
73 Toward the sheltered side

DOWN

1 Father of Leah and Rachel
2 Full of wrath
3 "The Karate Kid" actor
4 Less certain
5 "La-la" lead-in
6 Punjabi princess
7 In ___ (untidy)
8 Allowing seepage
9 Saucer pilot
10 What a certain octagonal sign requires
11 Gen. Robt. ___
12 Wimp
15 Talks back to
21 Sound from a mad cat
23 "Elder" or "Younger" Roman
25 Singer Rawls
28 Yearbook signers (Abbr.)

Puzzle 66 by Jim Page

31 Groundbreaker
32 "___ of the Road" (Boyz II Men hit)
34 "The Raven" author
36 2000 home run champ for the Cubs
37 Submissions to eds.
38 Kwik-E-Mart owner
39 Air passage
41 Finder of secrets
44 Instrument King David played
45 Earthquakes
47 Date

48 Where the Storting sits
51 Bronze coin of Spain
53 Emanating from stars
54 It has an eye, but it sees not
56 Formed into a circle
57 "What a pity!"
59 Irregular, as leaf edges
60 Waffles brand
61 Hockey shot
62 Wise, as advice
66 Yen fraction

I'LL DRIVE

ACROSS

1 Kind of market or media
5 Acapulco abode
9 Oscar Madison, for one
13 "I could ___ horse!"
14 Like some Vatican bulls
15 "Animal House" costume
16 First king of Israel
17 Encompassing everything
18 Surrounding glow
19 Be in the driver's seat
22 Conductance unit
23 Add the audio
24 Do an impression of
27 Cherry handle
30 Dish for serving soup
35 ". . . to thine own ___ be true"
37 Pub potables
39 "___ for Five" (1983)
40 Be in the driver's seat
43 "Caribbean Queen" singer Billy
44 "___ Brockovich"
45 Vending machine feature
46 Game that starts with love?
48 Words with "equal basis" or "upswing"
50 "Jeopardy" ques.
51 Vivacious actress West
53 Exec.'s degree, perhaps
55 Be in the driver's seat
64 It may be restricted

65 "___ and his money . . ."
66 "___, Caesar!"
67 "The Lion King" baddie
68 Hayley or Juliet
69 European volcano
70 Sibilant summons
71 Nickname of a cinematic Jones
72 Make judgments

DOWN

1 Ensnare
2 Great report card marks
3 R sequels?
4 "The House of the Seven Gables" locale
5 "Mondo ___" (1963)
6 On ___ with (about the same as)
7 Dressing may make it better
8 The exception is
9 "___ Trek: Deep Space Nine"
10 Look angry or sullen
11 Fairy-tale monster
12 False god mentioned in Judges
14 Crucial
20 Fun house cries
21 Shares a border with
24 "My Fair Lady" race place
25 Sign of the '60s?
26 "Sea of Love" star Barkin

Puzzle 67 by Ron Halverson

28 Vogue's newsstand neighbor
29 1997 Eddie Murphy film
31 Sideline cheers
32 Deadly African virus
33 Bernie's partner in songwriting
34 They're for the birds
36 Custard-filled tart
38 Climb, as a pole
41 Persona's opposite
42 Canine coats
47 Italian deli item

49 Major broadcaster
52 Like Santa's helpers
54 Oohed and ___
55 Barn door fastener
56 Tolkien monsters
57 Pastoral expanses
58 It has feathers and flies
59 "Lies My Father ___ Me" (1975)
60 "Monty Python and the ___ Grail"
61 Assign a "PG-13," e.g.
62 Chow down with class
63 Put down harshly

HOLDING THE BAG

ACROSS

1 On the say-so of
6 Punta del ___
10 "Amen" deacon
14 Irritate by rubbing
15 Sear, as a steak
16 Gamboling places
17 "I'm ___ here!" (skedaddler's cry)
18 Indian Head pennies, etc.
20 "A Nightmare on Elm Street" creator Craven
21 Small amount of money
23 Abominable snowman
25 Sportscast tidbit
26 Chip off the old flock?
28 Maiden-named
31 Moderately warm
35 Noted first name in jazz
36 Numbers for crunching, e.g.
38 Rubbish
39 Laila's father
40 Seafood cookout
42 "For Me and My ___"
43 It can be past or present
45 Ran full tilt
46 Bug bomb target
47 Display disdain
48 Costa del ___
49 "Friends" role
50 Presidencies, to historians
53 Way to decrease?
55 Unexpected blow

60 Identify, in a way
63 Type of letter
64 Word with "soap" or "horse"
66 "Believe ___ Not!"
67 Icelandic poetry collection
68 "___ for Murder"
69 Eighty-six
70 Diary starter
71 Vaulted settings

DOWN

1 "Don't have ___" (Bart Simpson quote)
2 "Leaving Las Vegas" actress
3 "Crazy" crooner
4 Newt wannabe
5 Punch back instinctively
6 Neutral shade
7 Pillow cover
8 They roll on baseball fields
9 Build, as a building
10 Oft-relocated employee
11 It's often controlling
12 Yin counterpart
13 Being, to Caesar
19 Extremely talkative
22 Language of India
24 Airport guesstimate, for short
26 They can be reserved
27 DeGeneres of talk
29 It once preceded Germany

30 Group character
32 Tropical legumes
33 Bridge declaration, perhaps
34 Shoulder muscles, to a bodybuilder
37 Bushy hairstyle
40 Actor Mel or Jose
41 Heirloom
44 "Georgy Girl" singers (with "The")
46 Paid player
51 Rainbow-shaped
52 Garden tool

54 Spin-off of "The Mary Tyler Moore Show"
55 Quarter deck?
56 Words with "the minute" and "date"
57 Some USN personnel
58 Stamp-of-approval letters
59 Approach
61 First name in courtroom fiction
62 Grable's trademarks
65 Die spot

WEARING SHADES

ACROSS

1 Your's might need to be cleaned up
4 Ceases moving
9 Like waves of grain
14 George Bush once headed it
15 Not just up
16 Mediterranean nation
17 Jaywalker's nemesis
18 Short-order order
20 Champagne salutes
22 Hatchet relative
23 Brides' escorts, usually
24 Amanda of "The Whole Nine Yards"
26 Expressed in writing
28 Easy, unobstructed progress
33 Valentine's Day symbol
34 Broad smiles
35 Throng
38 Horrible boss
39 "Peer Gynt" composer
40 Disney fish
41 Balloon's demise
42 Unrefined
43 Sub device
44 What many graduates look forward to
46 Barber belt
48 Celestial sights
49 Home to a prolific old woman
50 Largest book of the O.T.
53 Affirm
57 Good host's offering
60 What a milker's cold hands may cause
61 Tailors do it often
62 Wiser companion
63 Sidekick
64 Minute
65 You may provide a bed for one
66 Guileful

DOWN

1 What to make a dep. into
2 Arrivederci kin
3 O'Hara's fictional place
4 2004 speaker of the house
5 Mishandles or mistreats
6 "Man of a Thousand Faces" Chaney
7 Skipjack or bluefin
8 River way down under
9 Jack Horner's last words
10 Rabies victim
11 Sound off sheepishly?
12 Recital piece
13 Knocks
19 Home Economics class activity
21 Have mercy on
25 Riffraff
27 ICU workers
28 Ninja's motion

Puzzle 69 by Lynn Lempel

29 Small construction block
30 Wyatt, the old-time lawman
31 Type of whiskey
32 Misleads, in a way
35 Chef's compilation
36 Actor Sharif
37 Tedious type
39 Influenza
40 "You're wrong!"
42 ___-Magnon man
43 Undermine
44 Major West German port

45 Lens holders
46 Mud, after centuries
47 Egg-laden dessert
49 Hit the buzzer?
51 Plod through the mud
52 Legal org. co-founded by Jane Addams
54 Ballpark bosses
55 Certain global warming culprit
56 Divine
58 Sardonic
59 Lines of homage, collectively

IDOLIZED

ACROSS

1 Feed feasters for a fee
6 Chairwoman's address
11 Indianapolis dome
14 Lacking enthusiasm
15 Word with "zinc"
16 Popular November tuber
17 Famous fairgoer
19 "Wheel of Fortune" buy, sometimes
20 Follows suit
21 Airs or numbers
23 South of the border shawls
27 Den mother
29 Lift to your final destination?
30 Keanu's cinematic playground
31 Sesame Street resident
32 Gives up control
33 "The Office" character
36 Elton John's Broadway hit
37 City of witch hunts
38 Cat rescue site
39 "30 Rock" star
40 Brother of Moses
41 People of action
42 Tet Offensive city
44 Realm of Cyrus the Great
45 What army is for Mary
47 Cooks in liquid after browning
48 Plays the hero
49 It moves with runners
50 Classic TV mom Morgenstern
51 Start of a 1963 hit song

58 Archaeological excavation
59 Pakistan's river
60 Part of FAQ
61 Before, to the Bard
62 Fence adjuncts
63 Base negotiating amounts

DOWN

1 "60 Minutes" network
2 "When We Were Kings" profilee
3 ___-o'-shanter (Scottish cap)
4 Sixth sense
5 Bump on the road to recovery
6 Famous painting Grandma
7 X or y, e.g.
8 Not quite Mensa material
9 Hustle and bustle
10 Gives guidance
11 Nickname for a Hall of Famer Nolan's fastball
12 Striped candy
13 Haywire
18 Olympics sport
22 Prefix with "corn" or "start"
23 Reaper's bundle
24 Causing butterflies
25 "Macho Man" of wrestling
26 Soprano's solo, at the opera
27 Carrying a full load

Puzzle 70 by A.J. Mass

28 Part of a supermarket list
30 Crenshaw or casaba, e.g.
32 Bank shot, in billiards
34 Where the eagle has landed?
35 Tablelands
37 "The Forsyte ___" (Galsworthy)
38 A famous Amos
40 Zeppelin, e.g.
41 Like Steven Wright's delivery
43 It comes before beauty

44 Bugs, to Elmer
45 Dialogue that breaks the fourth wall
46 The low point
47 Graceful word?
49 Eyelid position
52 Music producer Brian
53 Gains by RBs
54 Peer Gynt's mother
55 Big Island instrument, briefly
56 Brought, as a horse to water
57 Super Bowl clips

A FULL DAY

ACROSS

1 1998 Robin Williams character, ___ Adams
6 Word after "or" in an ultimatum
10 Petty squabble
14 See ya in Hawaii?
15 They catch acrobats, on a bad day
16 Word in the title of a Chan / Tucker buddy film
17 Piece of history or Linda Hunt film "The ___"
18 Caustic substances
19 The "A" in A.D.
20 1971 Richard Thomas movie based on a novel of the same name
23 Like "Night Gallery" or Stephen King stories
24 Rubber-stamps
25 "My Little Chickadee" star
28 Vrooms or guns it
30 43,560 square feet
31 Grace under pressure
33 Merv Griffin tune, "___ Got a Lovely Bunch of Coconuts"
36 1975 Al Pacino classic
40 Nixon's start and finish?
41 "Flying Dutchman" actress Bergen
42 Not in favor of
43 Secretive "Hey, you there"
44 Brought a smile or giggle to
46 "O Come Let Us ___ Him"
49 "To be - to be" link
51 Title for the film and for Billy Crystal in a 1992 motion picture
57 Long, long geological time
58 What Mama did, according to the Shirelles
59 More standoffish or worse for winter driving
60 Type of radio or daytime show
61 Decorative holder of combs, perfumes, etc.
62 "Hotel California" group member
63 Mid-March date
64 Moore of the Emilio Estevez film, "Bobby"
65 "Ghostbusters" goo

DOWN

1 Henry VIII's sixth wife
2 On the safe side, at sea
3 Spoiled the surprise
4 Swindled, or used a carpenter's tool
5 Broke through a computer's security code
6 Former Chinese premier Zhou
7 Philippines island that was the site of a MacArthur victory
8 Part of a mushroom or rose
9 Exxon's old name
10 It may be given before a meal
11 Ancient Greek region called "the birthplace of philosophy"
12 What a stand-up comic better be
13 Kermit and a plague in the book of Exodus
21 Soph, jr. and sr.
22 Lunar ___ (Apollo 15 vehicle)
25 Screenwriter's instruction, "___ to black"
26 Computer desktop symbol
27 These work units are divisions of joules
28 Michael Caine "educated" her in a film
29 Suffix with "legal" or "Taiwan"
31 Huff and puff like a boxer?
32 Frequently, poetically

33 Particles that have their pluses and minuses
34 Show your hand during a showing of hands
35 Wife of Geraint in King Arthur lore
37 Valuable possession or annual report item
38 "Owner of a Lonely Heart" group
39 Relating to or involving ships or seamen
43 Short-sheeting, "Do you have Prince Albert in a can," etc.
44 First word in the title of a Jamie Foxx, Al Pacino football film

45 Peso, peseta, dollar, cent, euro, etc.
46 Teacher of Stradivari or the violin that bears his name
47 Fearful feeling
48 "___ Mio" (Dean Martin hit song)
49 Intense hatred
50 Diameter halves
52 Got some mileage out of
53 Assign a "PG-13" to
54 Classic Leslie Caron film
55 Big wheel at sea?
56 Gordon Parks' 1969 drama, "The Learning ___"

FOOD FUN

ACROSS

1 Parisian parent
5 Boss in the kitchen
9 Fly-catching bird
14 Alack partner
15 Deli sub
16 Aussie gems
17 Delivery vehicles
18 Diarist Frank
19 Some are hard to swallow
20 Goodman's sweet musicmaker
23 Lennon's lady
24 Loneliest number
25 Loafer's cushion
28 What vs. stands for
30 Kilmer of "The Saint"
32 By means of
33 Related, on mom's side
35 Ugly weather
37 Old-style advertising medium
40 Small bodies of water
41 Central American pyramid builders
42 Back, on a ship
43 Feminine pronoun
44 Mad magazine's genre
48 Capital of Nationalist China
51 Stones' hit, "___ Off My Cloud"
52 Part of HBO
53 Lady's application, perhaps
57 On or ___
59 Miser's pronoun
60 Thereabouts
61 Paramedics are trained to search for it
62 Screen image
63 Short comedy routines
64 Middle Eastern ruler
65 Three-handed card game
66 "At ___, soldier!"

DOWN

1 Dog researcher of note that caused many to salivate
2 Jerry's friend on "Seinfeld"
3 Long-lasting resentment
4 Exxon, once
5 Logger's tool
6 For that reason
7 Bald eagle's cousin
8 Batman and the Joker, e.g.
9 Appear uninvited
10 "How the West Was Won" and others
11 Uncontested win in a competition
12 Allen wrench shape
13 Man of Steel monogram
21 Prize fight divisions
22 "Shop ___ you drop"
26 Perjured oneself
27 "I could ___ a horse!"
29 Fax function

Puzzle 72 by Pamela Peterson

30 Church official
31 Needing kneading, maybe
34 It heals all wounds
35 Moonlight for Beethoven
36 Worst finish
37 Emergency guest bed
38 South, to the North
39 Cellar
40 "Wheel of Fortune" host Sajak
43 Cup preceder?
45 Gibraltar's peninsula

46 Drives, as from bed
47 Bring to light
49 Button on a DVD player
50 Keyboard key
51 Hometown of Christopher Columbus
54 "Jake's Thing" author Kingsley
55 Chorus line maneuver
56 Bryant of the Lakers
57 "The Murders in the Rue Morgue" beast
58 Thumb a ride

THAT HURTS!

ACROSS

1 Floor or roof squares
6 Show signs of life
10 Starting place for all of us
14 Oak, in a nutshell
15 Pitch
16 Side by side?
17 Roberts of "The Mexican"
18 Circle components
19 Not left out (Abbr.)
20 "Ask for a time-out!"
23 "___ the Good Times Roll"
26 "Some ___ It Hot" (1959 Marilyn Monroe film)
27 Amphitheaters
28 Slip away, as time
30 Opinionated equine
31 Snooty attitudes
32 Respond to stimuli
34 Hamm of soccer
37 "Get the music playing!"
41 The Say ___ Kid (Willie Mays)
42 Jennifer Garner series
43 Compressed data
44 Type of muffin
45 More tense
47 Like this clue
50 Coating of ice or frost
52 It can follow "you"
53 "Surf the big wave!"
56 Starting gate at Pimlico
57 Shakespearean character
58 Very small amounts
62 Cleveland's lake
63 "Braveheart" group
64 Harsh Athenian lawgiver
65 "___ I say more?"
66 "The ___ of Katie Elder"
67 Revises crossword clues

DOWN

1 ___ Mahal
2 Hospital area, for short
3 "Ha ha!" on the Internet
4 "CHiPS" actor Estrada
5 Slow-moving mollusks
6 Celery stem
7 Rich cake
8 Rainfall measure
9 Kind of grant
10 Imitated a siren
11 "Smoking ___?"
12 Spiritual center of Islam
13 Pitchers' illegal moves
21 Tell it like it isn't
22 Largest Greek island
23 Canine restraint
24 The best and the brightest
25 Lollygag
29 23rd Greek letter
30 Wrestling pads

Puzzle 73 by Carl Cranby

32 Completely botch
33 Fed. smog watchdog
34 Beatle suffix
35 Surmise
36 Think the world of
38 Limestone cavern phenomenon
39 Rubber bands and other assorted stretchy stuff
40 Oversized
44 Started, as a computer
45 Tall flightless bird
46 Treat with contempt

47 Place where many go downhill
48 Laundry or mowing the lawn, e.g.
49 Famous riveter or O'Donnell of talk
50 A daughter of King Lear
51 Elvis and Marilyn, e.g.
54 Angel costume accessory
55 "Hawaii Five-O" star
59 Mai ___ cocktail
60 Work as a thespian
61 Mayday letters

HAPPY BIRTHDAY!

ACROSS

1 Repairs, as a roof or road
5 "B.J. and the Bear" sheriff
9 Squirrel treat
14 Having or resembling wings
15 Melville's classic sequel to "Typee"
16 Off-limits
17 Steppenwolf 1968 hit
20 Steam train sound
21 Bourbon Street vegetable
22 Animal in a kid's song
23 Sounds of sorrow
24 You might have a stake in it
25 Buddhist religious center in Japan
27 It may be heard in an aviary
31 19th-century mail transport
33 Extinct bird
34 Emulate the hare of a famous fable
35 Hawaiian flower gift
36 Diller's spouse, affectionately
37 No longer divided
38 Nickname for a joker
42 Scuba gear
44 Eagle's nest
45 Meal remains
46 E-mail in-box nuisance
47 Like some small, seasonal, North pole workers
50 Relative of etc.
51 "Game, ___, and match"
54 Possible loan enders
57 Arab chieftain
58 Obsolete VCR format
59 A Sinatra
60 Dependent
61 Civic boundaries?
62 "A ___ Is Born"

DOWN

1 Hats for Scots
2 Word of woe
3 ___ to riches
4 ___ Lanka
5 Portable security device
6 Actors Epps and Sharif
7 When doubled, a Polynesian island
8 Alley-___ (basketball play)
9 Is present at
10 Gem measures
11 Kimono sashes
12 Was a passenger
13 "The First ___" (Christmas tune)
18 Journalist Alistair
19 Some still-life subjects
23 Isle of ___, Scotland
24 Promotional link

Puzzle 74 by Tracey Snyder

25 Not you, I or them
26 Not the big picture?
27 Makes coffee or beer
28 Muscateer?
29 Occasion at hand
30 British general in America, Thomas
31 Truck attachment
32 They often have twists
36 Lawyer employer
38 Perfunctory
39 Kind of print, briefly
40 Tropical fruits
41 Ruled territory

43 In need of laundering
46 One of fifty, in America
47 Bacheller's "___ Holden"
48 Flimsy, as excuses go
49 Cut and run
50 Fencing sword
51 Agitated state
52 Volcanic mount
53 Title for Ivan
55 Peacock network
56 Sci-fi figures

THINGS TO DO

ACROSS

1 Comments to a doctor
5 It'll hold water
9 Style is important here
14 Heavy blow
15 "E.R." actor Wyle
16 "Fantasy Island" sighting
17 Overlay, as macadam
18 Granny Smith throwaway
19 Start of a famous Schwarzenegger quote
20 Blood pressure raiser
21 Emulate a director?
23 Official population count
25 Bleak and desolate
26 Fable monsters
28 Shrimp habitat
32 Some artists' studios
34 "___ mouth, insert foot"
37 Revealing work of art?
38 Zoo attraction
39 Exertions
42 Chinese cosmic principle
43 It's drawn with a rifle?
45 Habitat
46 Duke of TV and film
48 Manuscript copyist
50 Mormon founder
52 Another part of 19-Across
55 Adjusts, as a suit
58 Emulate a skydiver?

62 A fixed charge for services
63 Conspicuous
64 Steal money or the money stolen
65 Wear a hole in the rug
66 Dentist's direction
67 Kind of wolf
68 London transportation
69 Michaelmas daisy
70 Runners support it
71 They travel with the band

DOWN

1 Tomato salad
2 Cognizant of one's surroundings
3 Emulate a superhero?
4 Jeanne d'Arc's title, briefly
5 Sheathe
6 Word with "steel" or "virgin"
7 British peers
8 Mitchell's Butler
9 Area of influence
10 Like a malamute
11 Corporal punishment unit
12 Clued-in regarding
13 With no ice
21 Invoke misfortune
22 "___ he grown!"
24 York or Pepper (Abbr.)
27 Three-seater, often

Puzzle 75 by Ron Halverson

29 Emulate a sharecropper?
30 Cut features
31 ". . . which nobody can ___"
32 Science class adjuncts
33 Trade org. since 1960
35 Starchy dish
36 Makes a muff
40 Type of wound
41 Restaurant faux pas
44 Heterogeneous
47 Sprint alternative
49 Not at all sweet

51 Soda fountain offering
53 Goes public
54 "___ and his money . . ."
56 Condensed wrap-up
57 "___ Like Old Times"
58 Part of a WWII exclamation
59 Nero's bird
60 "Daily Planet" reporter
61 First-class
65 Harper Valley org.

CLASSIC FILMS

ACROSS

1 Barney on "The Simpsons," for one
4 It has a point
9 Ambergris source
14 ___ for the books
15 Suggestion box fill
16 A status symbol
17 Asimov book that became a sci-fi classic
20 Arena parts
21 Pulitzer-winning columnist Herb
22 Setting for many jokes
23 "A" or "an"
26 Pot-bellied pet
27 PC key
28 De Niro film of '90
31 Battering device
34 Jack Benny's 39
35 Abominable snowmen
38 Commiserator's word
40 Floor models
43 Relinquish
44 One of Zeppo's brothers
46 Tiny Tim's instrument, briefly
47 Caviar, e.g.
48 1964 Best Picture
53 Fifth sign
55 Chinchilla's coat
56 Alarm clock, e.g.
60 Tabloid aviators, briefly
61 Bass or treble, e.g.
63 Sound beginning?
64 Film about a Little League team
68 Noted billionaire
69 Virus carrier, sometimes
70 Coxcomb
71 Surprise attack
72 Annie's pooch
73 Spider's parlor invitee

DOWN

1 Feature of the word "car" but not "cake"
2 Broadcasting
3 Basic principle
4 Total disaster
5 Pitched messages
6 Track record?
7 Worldly rather than spiritual
8 Con's preoccupation
9 Bad way to be convicted
10 Today, in Madrid
11 Statue material, perhaps
12 Word with "tender" or "aid"
13 Exercise, as influence
18 "What's your sine?" subj.
19 One of seven, to Salome
24 Washday unit

Puzzle 76 by Mabel Greene

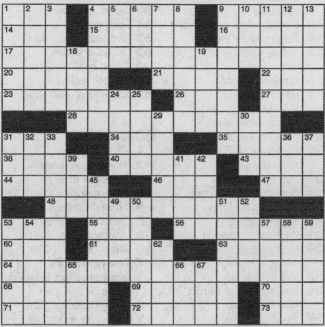

25 Part of a blade
29 Biggest human bone
30 Former nuclear agcy.
31 Bit of a cheer
32 ___ mode
33 Long-tailed South
American monkeys
36 Wedding promise
37 Come to understand
39 Operative
41 Sooners' st.
42 Seal in the juices
45 Thrown aside
49 "___ Lang Syne"

50 Cara and Castle
51 Twofold or a
way to be sure
52 Type of log
53 Fire, euphemistically
54 "___ Frome"
57 Type of car
or nurse
58 Filmdom's Flynn
59 Unpleasantly grating
62 Disaster-relief org.
65 It may sting a little
66 Obi-___ Kenobi
67 Caesar's first name

BERRY, BERRY GOOD

ACROSS

1 Classroom spinner
6 Espouses
10 Rounds, clips and such
14 Perceived by the ear
15 Salute with enthusiasm
16 Lender's security
17 8100 or 5810 Wireless, e.g.
20 Display the blues
21 Geographic area
22 Opposite of separateness
23 Pub measure
25 Safecracker, in slang
27 Wear by rubbing
30 Barley beards
31 Pet Rock, famously
34 Harry Potter's nemesis Malfoy
35 Wildly excited
36 Predecessor of Nadia and Mary Lou
37 Jim's raft mate
40 They're white in Monopoly
41 Propane holder
42 More than occasionally
43 Massachusetts Cape
44 Assault like a goat
45 Definitely not come-as-you-are
46 Cheese for crackers
47 "___ there, done that"
48 Native American home, stereotypically
51 Unstable subatomic particle
53 ___ gin fizz

57 Place immortalized by the Beatles
60 Soon, ere now
61 Take apart
62 Shaped like an egg
63 St. Louis eleven
64 "Star Trek" phaser setting
65 Columbus' hometown

DOWN

1 Chews the fat
2 Remarkable person, object or idea
3 Face-to-face exam
4 Hikers' burdens
5 Yellowstone beast
6 Alternative to white or rye
7 Lost pencils are sometimes found behind these
8 Villain's doing
9 Stallone's nickname
10 Word with "move," "tag" or "string"
11 Modest skirt length
12 Make the acquaintance of
13 "For Your Eyes ___"
18 Nota ___
19 Coffee containers
24 Graven image
26 Ga. Tech grad
27 Committee type
28 Shoe designer Magli
29 Hurried
30 Word with "free" or "secret"

Puzzle 77 by Donna S. Levin

31 Emulates a butterfly
32 "___ of God,"
   play and movie
33 Thomas or Kaye
35 Reprieve from a tax
   obligation
36 Like some football
   tackles or guards
38 Small toiletry case
39 Time long past
44 Steep, as tea
45 ". . . which nobody
   can ___"
46 Green and lima

47 Atomic number 5
48 Romanov ruler
49 Destructive peak
   in Sicily
50 Senior celebration
52 Official language
   of Pakistan
54 "Mila 18" author Uris
55 Hodgepodge
56 Norse literary
   collection
58 Partridge Family vehicle
59 A pilot may wait
   for it to lift

CLEAN IT UP

ACROSS

1 Feudal groundskeepers
6 "Charlie's Angels" actress
10 "What's the big ___?"
14 Become dangerous for driving
15 Sam Shepard's award
16 Goes to low beam, e.g.
17 Rock concert venue
18 Word in a Neil Diamond song title
19 Lob trajectories
20 American blues legend
23 Leaves in the bag?
24 Close hermetically
25 Played for time
27 Spearheaded
30 "Fiddlesticks!"
32 Every partner
33 In addition
35 Outback avians
37 Person in a palace
40 Struggle for breath
41 Pop and jerk
43 Highchair feature
44 Starts the pot
46 Toothbrush type
47 Lake near Niagara Falls
48 Jabbers
50 Boned up on
52 Fabric amts.
53 A-mazing creatures?
56 It may wear down after too much travel
58 Cordon bleu's phrase

59 "Who's Afraid of Virginia Woolf?" Oscar winner
64 Have good feelings about
66 Signify
67 Remark to the audience
68 Genesis casualty
69 Blanch
70 Russian roulette bet?
71 Strong and lean
72 Short play
73 Words of agreement

DOWN

1 Where Anna met the king
2 Neutral shade
3 Stalk by the river
4 Backs with bucks
5 Homophone for spade
6 Home of the A-bomb
7 Lie adjacent to
8 Feasted
9 Collegian's quest
10 She's "sweet as apple cider"
11 San Francisco cop of film
12 One who gets on with the show
13 Syria's president
21 Peddler's load
22 Smelting waste
26 Sharp

Puzzle 78 by Lynn Lempel

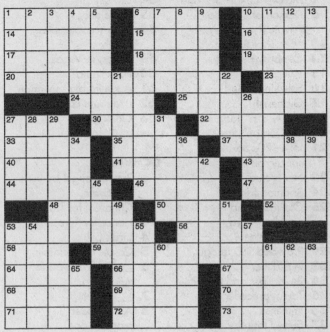

27 Org. to keep women on course?
28 Flair
29 Former Giants manager
31 British royal family
34 Ancient weapon
36 One's savings, metaphorically
38 Bookie's fear
39 Easter supplies
42 Hardly cutting-edge
45 They give you a soaking

49 By-the-book purchase
51 Gloomy
53 Dey legal-eagle drama
54 Cover story
55 Underhanded one
57 Come as a consequence
60 Painter of melted watches
61 Pen points
62 Wait curbside
63 Gets an eyeful
65 TV Tarzan actor

WILLY-NILLY

ACROSS
1 Maxwell Smart, for one
6 Damon of "Saving Private Ryan"
10 "___ That Tune"
14 Celebrity bit part
15 Winglike
16 Folk singer Burl
17 Gibberish
19 "M*A*S*H" lodging
20 TV "Tarzan" Ron
21 '50s–'70s Soviet spacecraft series
22 Not factual
24 Brighton farewell
25 Old-fashioned wedding word
26 Public esteem
29 Projected 3-D image
33 In a dither
34 Be in class and miss it
35 Tat-tat preceder
36 Immense
37 Sorted laundry accumulations
38 Bowie's model wife
39 Sparkling wine city
40 Robert of "The Brady Bunch"
41 Mom and pop may run one
42 Handbills
44 Does the job effectively
45 Goes to waste, in a way
46 Theater trophy
47 Fill, as with a certain quality
50 Puppies' plaints

51 Live ___ (1985 concert)
54 Classify
55 Timid one
58 High schooler's test, briefly
59 Bones, in Vegas
60 Fatty liquid
61 Abominable snowman
62 Bedframe component
63 On edge

DOWN
1 Brand bought by Wile E. Coyote
2 Conquest for Caesar
3 Honor for "Frasier"
4 Bird's bill
5 Carole King classic
6 ___ Loa, Hawaiian volcano
7 ___ mater
8 A bartender may run one
9 Ills
10 The heart of the matter
11 Assert
12 Diner's card
13 Princely Italian family
18 Burlap material
23 Keanu in "The Matrix"
24 Ice cream choice
25 Seeped
26 Monopolist's lack
27 Clear the slate
28 Linguine, e.g.
29 Argument flaws or 2003 Shia LaBeouf film

Puzzle 79 by Ron Halverson

30 Aquino's successor as Philippine president
31 Classic video game name
32 French impressionist artist Édouard
34 Heavyweight plans?
37 Fakes it
41 Solar blot
43 ___ Alamos
44 Reprint
46 "Seven Years in ___" (Pitt film)

47 Cosby/Culp series
48 Jimmy Durante trademark
49 "Animal House" house
50 It starts, "Young man, there's no need to feel down"
51 Church congregation's response
52 Wading bird
53 Unit of force
56 Be unwell
57 Hearty pub offering

PUTTING ON A SHIRT

ACROSS

1 Bends under weight
5 Clinton's first Secretary of Labor
10 Org. for female fellowship
14 "Star ___" (Shatner show)
15 ___-Saxon
16 They catch waves
17 ". . . ___ saw Elba"
18 Some sporting animals
20 Puccini heroine
22 One of Santa's reindeer
23 Health resort
24 Illegal factory
26 Hauled
28 Chum
29 Defoe's Miss Flanders
30 Bright, as a pupil
33 Xerox again
37 Actress Scala and others
40 Captain Cook's discovery
43 Tiny energy source
44 Cave
45 Bradley and McMahon
46 Sorrowful sound
48 Sick
50 Pinewood Derby entrant
52 Male bodybuilder
58 "___ Beso" (1962 hit)
59 Bedside awakener
61 Hackneyed
62 Gridiron lineup, sometimes
65 Half a dual personality
66 It gets jumped
67 "Awesome!" in the fifties
68 Tucked in for the night
69 ". . . ___ I'm told"
70 Drained of color
71 Optometry product

DOWN

1 Leaves in, editorially
2 Straight as an ___
3 "Silly" birds
4 Aspen topper
5 Grammy category
6 Father of Methuselah
7 Arctic house
8 Walk noisily
9 Legendary funnyman Bob
10 Desire
11 Dieter's target
12 Blintz relative
13 Syrian president
19 Germany's von Bismarck
21 Home video game innovator
25 "Jingle Bells" vehicle
27 Gymnast Korbut
29 "___ Pizza" (1988)
30 "I knew it!"

Puzzle 80 by Lynn Lempel

31 Butter measure
32 Double ice cream order
34 Indy-winning vehicle
35 Noted bride of 1969
36 Seedy discard
38 Lengthen (with "to")
39 Flat tire sound
41 Parisian lady friend
42 Lazes about
47 Light metric weight
49 Deadly
50 Fashionably old-fashioned

51 "But ___ me, give me liberty . . ."
52 Chess victories
53 Heep, of "David Copperfield"
54 Hit, to King James
55 Noncommittal answer
56 Plymouth Colony leader
57 Essentials
60 "Sweater Girl" Turner
63 Rock's ___ Speedwagon
64 ___ sequitur

CONDIMENT TRAY

ACROSS
1 "___ the Tiger" (1973)
5 Partner of Clark or Martin
10 "That ___ Cat!" (1965)
14 Aglow
15 ___-Dale (Nottinghamshire resident)
16 Lamb's pen name
17 Home of "Stormy Weather" fame
18 Sour-faced one
20 Palindromic Devon river
21 "Vaya Con ___"
22 Ruling threesome
23 Emaciated
25 Part of a picket fence
26 Book with 150 chapters
28 Don't run with these
32 "Topper Takes ___" (1939)
33 "There's no ___ like home"
34 ___ de plume
35 Hindu prince's title
36 Neglect, as responsibilities
37 Kin of Rover and Spot
38 "___ e Leandro" (Mancinelli opera)
39 ". . . town, riding on ___"
40 Exult in winning
41 Scooping up a river bottom
43 Name of the first surviving quintuplets
44 Paddy product
45 Hummingbirds do it
46 Tarnish, as a reputation

49 Like a nursery rhyme cupboard
50 Phrase heard in court or church
53 Military uniforms
55 Refuse to acknowledge
56 River in a Christie title
57 Loosen a knot
58 Wrinkled fruit
59 "Ask me no questions and I'll ___ . . ."
60 Meat unit
61 ___ of Capri

DOWN
1 Ad come-on
2 "Jeopardy!" host Trebek
3 General Stilwell of WWII
4 Airport guesstimate, for short
5 Certain rabbits
6 "Silas Marner" novelist George
7 Some WWII service personnel
8 Cuttlefish excretion
9 Where animals may go for saline
10 Bus terminals
11 His, in Le Havre
12 Board game of world conquest
13 Spaced-out org.?
19 Expunge
21 "What a ___!" (Bette Davis quote)
24 Inter ___ (among other things)
25 Bone-chilling

Puzzle 81 by Frances Hansen

A crossword grid with numbered cells: 1, 2, 3, 4, 5, 6, 7, 8, 9, 10, 11, 12, 13, 14, 15, 16, 17, 18, 19, 20, 21, 22, 23, 24, 25, 26, 27, 28, 29, 30, 31, 32, 33, 34, 35, 36, 37, 38, 39, 40, 41, 42, 43, 44, 45, 46, 47, 48, 49, 50, 51, 52, 53, 54, 55, 56, 57, 58, 59, 60, 61.

26 Downsized
27 Brenda or Bart
28 Arm supporter
29 French fries alternative
30 Tokyo trasher, in a '50s film
31 Dealt a mighty blow
33 Word with "tag" or "booth"
36 Enlivened, in a way
37 Drifting ice sheet
39 Twinkle-toed
40 "___ me your tired, your poor . . ."
42 Gibberish
43 Bandleader Jimmy or Tommy
45 Behavioral pattern
46 One word of advice
47 "Night" author Wiesel
48 "___ 'er up!"
49 Sheet of matted cotton, e.g.
51 Humdrum
52 Off-Broadway award
54 Genetic inits.
55 Start for juris or generis

JUST LEAVE ALREADY

ACROSS

1 Western film
6 Sound in body
10 Elite police team
14 Address an audience
15 "Potpourri for 1000, ___"
16 Apple leftover
17 Leave quickly
19 You'll get credit for it
20 End of a campus e-mail address
21 Type of child
22 A prayer
24 Expel from America
26 Damascus resident
27 Leave quickly
33 Doesn't just sniffle
36 Flies off the handle
37 Steak partner
38 Bargain spread
39 Quoted as an authority
40 Farm implement
41 "___ on a Grecian Urn"
42 Golf club socket
43 "Thanks, but I've already ___"
44 Leave quickly
47 Pretentiously cultured
48 Ascending
52 Amati of violin-making fame
55 Greek god of love
57 A deer, a female deer
58 "Man on the ___" (1999)
59 Leave quickly
62 Do lawn work
63 Distinctive flair
64 "Cheers" character
65 "___ I say more?"
66 Smooth fabric
67 Smooths the path

DOWN

1 ___ and aahed
2 Thumb ___ (hitchhike)
3 Advance after a catch, in baseball
4 Suffix with some ordinal numbers
5 Snappy comebacks
6 Weather forecast, perhaps
7 Treaty brother
8 Wahine wear
9 Demanded a ransom, e.g.
10 Book copier of old
11 Romances
12 First name in folk music
13 Suffix for four
18 Get the pot going
23 Cheerleaders' cheers
25 Capital of Norway
26 Turner portrayer Bassett
28 Straight-laced and then some

29 Granola-like	**45** Brought in, as a salary
30 "Atlas Shrugged" hero	**46** Seniors' last dance?
31 Cosmetics additive	**49** Gray matter output
32 No longer bursting at the seams?	**50** Herman's Hermit
33 Sound of thunder	**51** Twins share them
34 Burghoff's co-star	**52** Parishioner's word
35 10,080 minutes	**53** Botanical joint
39 Small country houses	**54** Chief magistrate of Venice
40 Settles a debt	**55** Etc. relative
42 Fire antonym	**56** Social standing
43 Sitcom installment	**60** Wallach in "The Two Jakes"
	61 Route word

SOME THINGS ARE FREE

ACROSS

1 "I Love Lucy" regular
6 Display intense anger
10 Greek salad ingredient, perhaps
14 "___ Sixteen" (Ringo Starr hit)
15 "___ out?" (poker dealer's query)
16 Novelist Turgenev or the "The Terrible"
17 Two FREE things
20 Punctured ball sound
21 Evicts
22 Homer's honey
23 Kind of screen
24 Advocating
25 Quivering trees
28 Discuss
33 One-time pupa
34 Imaginary narrative
35 Whitney or Wallach
36 Three FREE things
40 Beast of burden
41 Knee-slapper
42 A&M student
43 Val Kilmer film
46 Grounds for divorce, in some states
47 Blood letters
48 Prod, as with a finger
49 Lamp cover
52 Free-swinging affair
54 Where X marks the spot
57 Three FREE things
60 Toward the sheltered side
61 Diva's highlight
62 Can't help but
63 Bride's pride
64 Web sites?
65 Country singer Hoyt

DOWN

1 "The ___ have it"
2 Howard and Reagan
3 1987 Barbra Streisand movie
4 "You ___ So Beautiful"
5 Pinpoint
6 "Who's on ___ ?" (comedy routine)
7 Type of pricing
8 Forest undergrowth
9 Palindromist's preposition
10 Mozart subject
11 Penultimate fairy tale word
12 Apollo quaff
13 Get the pot going
18 Some crossword clues
19 Crazy way to run
23 Building toy
24 "One ___ Over the Cuckoo's Nest"
25 Set one's sights on
26 Shatter

Puzzle 83 by Mark Milhet

27 Behind the times
28 Deal of fortune?
29 Zillions
30 Brink
31 ___ Island, immigration station
32 Fair offers?
34 Dime description
37 Lounge group, sometimes
38 Wisconsin city
39 Shrek, e.g.
44 Depress
45 Genesis shepherd

46 Take-charge type
48 Skirt feature
49 Carpet type
50 Luminous topper
51 From square one
52 She ain't what she used to be
53 Emmy winner Falco
54 Classic computer game
55 Choir member
56 Lowly laborer
58 Lummox
59 Sales add-on

HALT!

ACROSS
1 Some Wharton grads
5 Persona non ___
10 Gumbo ingredient
14 Obi-Wan portrayer
15 "___ Without a Cause"
16 Tender meat
17 Poi ingredient
18 To a sailor's left
19 Bronte heroine
20 "That's enough!"
23 Bonehead's response
24 Strong desires
25 Aurora's counterpart
28 Rum-soaked cake
31 Stage whisper
34 Not in favor of
36 Actors McKellen and Holm
38 Sharp-billed wader
40 "Come no farther!"
43 Rich dessert cake
44 Place for a knot you cannot untie
45 Plane section
46 Acts like Tom?
48 They accompany turkey and dressing
50 Cartoon voice Blanc
51 It might be skipped
53 Epitome of easiness
55 "That's enough!"
62 Pinocchio, for one

63 Fitzgerald and Raines
64 "For heaven's ___!"
66 Pony up
67 Say "ouch!" when pinched, e.g.
68 Affirm with confidence
69 Annoying type
70 Maritime birds
71 Coniferous evergreens

DOWN
1 "Welcome" bearer
2 Rainy day feeling
3 Prefix for dynamics
4 Chide, as a child
5 Sign of maturity
6 Auto making a comeback?
7 "___ Ben Adhem"
8 "Waiting to Exhale" novelist McMillan
9 Tennis great Gibson
10 Mistake resulting from inattention
11 Super's collection
12 Nearly extinct
13 Hearty libations
21 Name, as a knight
22 Commencement
25 River in New York
26 "___ of Old Smoky"
27 Stop partner
29 Food on a hook

30 Like Sidney Lumet's twelve men
32 "All I Have to Do Is ___"
33 Unsettlingly strange
35 Translate
37 1969 World Series stadium
39 Blow the whistle
41 Stop on the line
42 Violent storms
47 Heavenly object
49 Bro counterpart

52 Conger chaser
54 English test requirement
55 Duel provoker
56 Meat stabber
57 Feedbag contents
58 Get ready for the wedding
59 Run for the money?
60 Roof repair site
61 Depict unfairly
65 Stammerer's syllables

IN COMMON

ACROSS

1 Everly Brothers hit
6 One with great power
10 Invitation letters
14 "Biography" network
15 It can be a lifesaver
16 Out of the wind
17 Type of political support
19 When many doors open
20 Egyptian cobra, e.g.
21 Boston music makers
22 Words with "arms" or "space"
24 Cuts inches off yards?
25 Is cautious of
26 Allows in
29 Rimes of country
30 A great number
31 Tranquility and Sargasso
32 Tap trouble
36 Gung-ho
37 Unsavory
38 Watch part
39 Convince
40 Baking measures
41 "Carmen" composer
42 Receives a stipend
44 Parking attendants
45 Cochise and Geronimo, e.g.
48 Learned
49 CPA's expertise
50 Refer to
51 CBS exec Moonves
54 Shake in the grass?
55 Ordinary people
58 Bullfighters' bravos
59 At the peak of
60 Andrews of "Mary Poppins"
61 Impertinent talk
62 Word with "tail" or "express"
63 Certain suite

DOWN

1 Narrative of heroic exploits
2 They make waves
3 Hike the ball
4 Consumer Reports lacks them
5 Strict taskmasters
6 Farmer's concerns
7 Some allow petting
8 Suited to the task
9 "Don't worry about a thing"
10 Union members
11 More conniving
12 Where the case is tried
13 Henhouse sounds
18 Noisy quarrels
23 Barley bristle
24 Like most of suburbia

Puzzle 85 by Merle Baker

25 Sweat particles
26 "Oh dear!"
27 Plunged downward
28 Word with "voice" or "express"
29 Some ballet moves
31 Has nothing to do with
33 Completely demolish
34 "Law & Order: SVU" actor
35 Motel bans, often
37 Pepsi bottle topper
41 Curly-tailed dog

43 "Gotcha!"
44 Don Corleone
45 Dumas character
46 First name among "American Idol" judges
47 Assembly line supply
48 Popeye's pal
50 "Let's go!"
51 Goof off
52 Lamb's "Essays of ___"
53 Depict unfairly
56 Plains people
57 Amusement

MATERIAL WORLD

ACROSS

1 Pet adoption grp.
5 Pool measurement
10 Hole punchers
14 Woeful expression
15 Irregularly notched
16 Hip
17 Printing process
19 Word with "dial" or "muscle"
20 Some Guernseys
21 Caught in the act
23 "We're number ___!"
24 Not digital
26 Gordon in "Oklahoma!"
29 Application request
32 Wall St. debut
33 Part of an October 31 phrase
35 Telephone button
36 The i's have it
37 Half a figure eight
38 "___ Gratia Artis" (MGM motto)
41 Good thing to give your child
42 Sciences counterpart
44 Renter's sign
46 Ancient Tokyo
47 Old interruption
50 Animal that drives rabbits from their homes
52 City on the Loire or NFL Hall of Famer Ernie
53 One of the Gabors
54 Corpus front
56 Utilized Lego blocks
60 Fired ruthlessly
61 Blue items, in a Presley song
64 Field rodent
65 "Dallas" matriarch Miss ___
66 "Cogito, ___, sum"
67 ___ 'acte (intermission)
68 Some turns or punches
69 With a discount of

DOWN

1 Window frame
2 Ballerina's knee bend
3 City in Colombia
4 Requisition
5 They make judicial decisions
6 Flubs it
7 "The Tell-Tale Heart" author
8 Mao ___-tung
9 Reddish dyes
10 They speak louder than words
11 Daydream
12 "The ___ Ranger"
13 Husky-powered vehicle
18 House companion
22 Computer keyboard key
24 Part of a recipe phrase
25 Birth-based

26 Man with a
golden touch
27 Opposite of starboard
28 Alabama, Georgia,
Arkansas, etc.
30 Norman Lear show
31 Disease of cereal
grasses
34 Perfumer's compound
39 One who separates
boxers
40 Canyon and Allen
43 State trooper's quarry
45 Choice conjunctions

48 Breakfast of
centurions?
49 Sailing ship
51 Jennifer on "Friends"
54 "___ Gun, Will Travel"
55 Nerve part
56 Delete a scene, e.g.
57 Barreled along
58 Brain test results,
for short
59 Brit. decorations
62 "Glob" or "mod"
attachment
63 Santa's little helper

TRY AGAIN

ACROSS

1 Pseudonym of H.H. Munro
5 "Pipe down!"
10 Proust novel "Remembrance of Things ___"
14 "___ Arms" (Journey hit song)
15 First of a series
16 Lumbago, e.g.
17 Pinto pusher?
20 Brush off
21 Sherman's maid on "The Jeffersons"
22 CPR pro
23 ___ de Cologne
25 Be inaccurate
27 Reunion neckwear?
34 To's reverse
35 Tollbooth location
36 Development developments
38 It's often masked
40 Napoli love
42 Tuning fork's output
43 Varnish ingredient
45 Ibsen's "An ___ of the People"
47 It's nailed
48 Where environmentalists put down their notes?
51 In the manner of
52 Alphabet sequence
53 Former airline
56 Prefix with -pedic
60 Smoldering coal
64 EPA concern
67 State pointblank
68 Susan Lucci role
69 Hemingway's posthumous "The Garden of ___"
70 "The ___ is history"
71 Back-to-school item
72 For fear that

DOWN

1 Like Aesop's grapes
2 Vaulted altar area
3 "___ on truckin'"
4 "Positively!"
5 Health farm
6 Stay out of its way!
7 Major in astronomy?
8 "The Evening ___" (1996)
9 Jewish foundation
10 Ballet step
11 Summit
12 Bedding item
13 Outdoor accommodation
18 Fastening device
19 Where to find everyone
24 Pauley Pavilion squad
26 Sing Sing disorder
27 Word with "tall" or "come to"
28 Almost ready for the tooth fairy
29 "Hill Street Blues" actress
30 Environmentalist's concern
31 Took part in a regatta

Puzzle 87 by Jim Page

32 Overdo it onstage
33 Spanish title
34 Supporting
37 Neither fold nor raise
39 Costa ___
41 Caligula and Napoleon, briefly
44 Billy Joel album "The ___ Curtain"
46 Eastwood in "Rawhide"
49 ID checker
50 Thrash
53 Anastasia's father, e.g.

54 "___ Got Tonight" (Bob Seger hit)
55 They're good for tricks
57 Traffic sign word
58 Flag Alex Rieger's vehicle
59 First word in a fairy tale
61 Forecast
62 Makes do (with "out")
63 Jonathan Larson's musical
65 Diner's snippet
66 ___ es Salaam

ALTERNATE SPELLING

ACROSS

1 Autumn pear
5 More than fervent
10 Finder's reward
13 "This man walks into ___ . . ." (start of some jokes)
14 Gives the slip
16 Careless
17 The next Michael Jordan?
19 One way to sell stocks, briefly
20 Connector of floors
21 "Enterprise" android
22 Family card game
23 Lillian or Dorothy of film
26 In a while
28 Fast poke
31 Least varying tide
33 Measure of sugar
34 Kate Hudson film of 2000
37 Music for a movie
40 "Buenos ___"
41 Exodus mountain
43 Ablutionary vessel
44 Everglades wader
46 Some messages are delivered on them
48 Country club charges
50 Cylindrical storage tower
51 Lobster coral
52 Huxley who wrote about Africa
55 Irish or Welsh ancestor
57 Bolt attachment
58 Nabisco cookie
60 Certain Middle Easterners
64 601, in old Rome
65 What you get when you cook the books?
68 Awkward person
69 Unimportant part of a speech or writing
70 Classic TV's "___ Room for Daddy"
71 Abbr. on an overdrawn account
72 Not you, I or them
73 get ready for surgery

DOWN

1 Statements from a black sheep
2 Death notice, for short
3 "___ Smile" (Hall & Oates hit)
4 Diet guru Jenny
5 Weight room unit
6 Ex-wife of Mickey and Frank
7 Poet of old
8 Perfect
9 One type of insurance
10 Mantra for a hippie baker?
11 "Jack Sprat could ___ . . ."
12 Released felon
15 Social standing
18 Computer command
24 Global seven

25 Seen enough
27 Quizmaster, e.g.
28 Green gemstone
29 "You're making ___ mistake!"
30 Rigid as a two-by-four?
32 Glass squares
35 Burn, as energy
36 Frenzied
38 Provide with a new look
39 Skye writing
42 Maroon's locale
45 Drive at Pebble Beach?

47 Word with "cap" or "bear"
49 Run through a sieve
52 Conclude with
53 "Star Wars" creator
54 Parrot's word
56 Beat the pants off
59 Munch Museum site
61 Way off yonder
62 Human-powered vehicle
63 How-to part
66 Bard's nightfall
67 Cautionary beginning?

CHANNEL SURFING

ACROSS

1 "Dick Tracy" gal
5 Mil. training class
9 "A likely story!"
12 Eye nerve
14 Geometry calculations
16 Matter of self-interest?
17 Delaying strategy
19 Set aflame
20 One supporting a habit?
21 Company that bought Time Warner
22 Goes ballistic
24 Big game?
26 Leather cleaner
29 Assaults olfactorily
31 It comes before a dropped name
32 Lincoln, for one
33 It may whiz past one's knees
35 Chaplin prop
38 Vietnamese holiday
39 Archivist's material
42 Lively dance
45 Sought damages from
46 Begs
50 Guthrie Center founder
52 ___ Moines, Iowa
54 Noted virologist and polio fighter Albert
55 Gracious winners, e.g.
59 "Friends" star Kudrow
60 Open, in a way
61 Tire support
63 One way to make a bough break

64 They may be ripped or crunched
65 Virginia shipbuilding center
69 "The Facts of Life" actress Charlotte
70 Challenged
71 Assistant who handles letters
72 Many SAT takers
73 Use an IBM Selectric, e.g.
74 Vanquish

DOWN

1 Word in the title of a Steve Martin/ Goldie Hawn film
2 Shoulder adornment
3 Bugs Bunny question that begins, "Ain't I a . . ."
4 Kennel order
5 Sweater style
6 End of some e-mail addresses
7 Japanese ceremonial drink
8 Bedouin transporter
9 Lend a hand
10 Stir up
11 Popular nightclub
13 KGB counterpart
15 Waterless
18 Discouraging words
23 It's in the heart of Jerusalem?
25 Read quickly

27 Reader of secret messages
28 Unhearing
30 Winter transports
34 Old gold coin
36 ___ in the bud
37 Wings on buildings
40 Overhaul
41 "You Can Call ___" (Paul Simon tune)
42 Jacksonville team
43 Jail cell feature
44 Women's lip applications
47 Site of the Eisenhower Library
48 Renounces
49 Speaks sharply to
51 Horace work, e.g.
53 Walked
56 Hourglass filler
57 Fabric fold
58 Business letter addressee, perhaps
62 Osbourne popularizer
66 Like some humor
67 Zing
68 Collar

DOWN ON THE FARM

ACROSS

1 Commercial-free network
4 ___ Picchu, Peru
9 Creature known for its keen vision
14 Wheat or white alternative
15 Where van Gogh lived for a while
16 With less moisture
17 45 inches, formerly
18 Kind of manual
19 Doomed one
20 Classic sports film
23 Very old
24 Oil-rich peninsula
27 Obsolete VCR format
28 Visited Davy Jones' locker, in a way
31 "Song ___ Blue" (Neil Diamond hit)
32 It comes before a dropped name
35 Spaghetti recipe word
37 "Norma ___" (1979)
38 William Faulkner work
41 Money player
43 Sources of problems for prima donnas
44 Restorative resort
45 Handle without care
47 Word with "bug" or "misty"
49 Growth on stones or receiver Randy
53 High-pitched in tone
55 Muse of lyric poetry
58 Donkey or ox, e.g.
61 Pirate's rum drinks
63 Fur trader John Jacob
64 The six of "Little Nellie Kelly"
65 Boleyn and Rice
66 Hopeless
67 Steak partner
68 Opera villain, often
69 Does a database chore
70 Timothy Leary stash

DOWN

1 Assembled in advance, as a home
2 Credit for a crossword constructor
3 Jukebox verb
4 Norman Lear show
5 Firebug's crime
6 Chin indentations
7 Bunch of cattle
8 Superpower until 1991
9 Poe or Degas
10 Starbucks emanations
11 A Supreme Court justice
12 "Enter the Dragon" star
13 Be imperfect
21 Amazon vine
22 "The Chess Players" painter Thomas
25 Once ___ lifetime

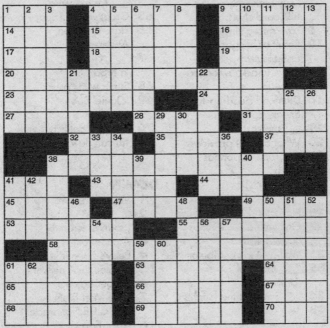

26 Wine improver
29 It voids warranties
30 Hide-hair link
33 Obsolete preposition
34 Marx colleague
36 It's right under
   your nose
38 Some whiskeys
39 Baby in blue
40 Title giver
41 Thatcher and
   Blair, briefly
42 It's a bit of cheer
46 Feudal lords

48 More adroit or skillful
50 Trying experience
51 Recites the letters
   of a word
52 Knew intuitively
54 Rodeo necessity
56 German craft
57 Ottoman Empire
   inhabitants
59 Starts a paragraph,
   electronically
60 Capital of Norway
61 Social one's gift
62 Genetic initials

OVERHEAD ITEMS

ACROSS

1 They make the Billboard charts
5 Low-voiced singers
10 Result of hunger or jealousy
14 Leave unacknowledged
15 Blow up
16 Diamond Head bash
17 Energy converters
19 ___ mater
20 What a ticket provides
21 Fragrant, poisonous shrub
23 Word with "for" or "white"
26 Newsstand offering
27 One with a flower fetish
31 Well-heeled contributor
35 "___ the Roof" (Drifters hit)
36 ___ Day and the knights
38 "A Whiter ___ of Pale" (1967 Procol Harum hit)
39 Man the bar
40 Webster and Beery
42 Washington notes
43 Lover's keepsake, perhaps
45 Support on stage?
46 Knucklehead
47 "___ Biggest Selection" (Amazon.com trademark)
49 Fit of rage
51 Occasion at Minsky's
53 Jackson Browne classic
54 Duly appointed agent
58 Pipsqueak

62 ". . . one giant ___ for mankind"
63 Great voids in space
66 Hans Christian Andersen, e.g.
67 "___ Grows in Brooklyn"
68 Suffix with "psych"
69 "Daniel Boone" actor Ed
70 Chicago political name
71 Tin can flaw

DOWN

1 Vacuum feature
2 "___ Fire" (Springsteen hit)
3 Arcade foul
4 Betsy's banner
5 "I, Claudius" network
6 Ginger adjunct
7 "The Man From U.N.C.L.E." character
8 Actor Eriq La ___
9 "We have nothing to fear but fear ___"
10 Trendy eatery chain
11 "___ Lang Syne"
12 "A Horse With No ___"
13 Cluster bean
18 Pitcher of seven no-hitters
22 Start of a phrase of regret
24 Monarch on all fours
25 Prohibit, legally
27 City in Montana
28 Passion of a noted phantom

29 Laser printer supply
30 Beauty queen adornment
32 It may get a good paddling
33 Between two intimate people
34 In a foul mood
37 Looks for bargains
41 Canine of kiddie literature
44 Casually catch flies
48 "Jingle All the Way" star

50 Ginger Rogers movie "The Primrose ___"
52 River part
54 Farr's sitcom co-worker
55 Sewer's union?
56 Clearheaded
57 ___ "The Pearl" Monroe
59 "What ___ can go wrong?"
60 Trigger puller?
61 Secretive attention getter
64 Fair grade
65 "The Star-Spangled Banner" lyricist

SMILES ALL AROUND

ACROSS

1 Astringent substance
5 Type of cheese
9 Break up, as a relationship
14 "Damn Yankees" girl
15 Sitting on
16 Cold-weather forest
17 After everyone else
18 Scuttlebutt
19 Exemplar of straightness
20 Novel and movie by Carl Reiner
23 "Fly Away Home" birds
24 Van Gogh had one later in life
25 Call ___ day
28 Make a mistake
29 All but one in a million?
33 Like some decisions
34 Stars with fluctuating brightness
35 Leaves the groom at the altar
36 "Bye Bye Birdie" hit
41 Revolted
42 Measuring instrument
43 "___ Rider" (Eastwood western)
44 Portable heat source
46 Nile Valley reptile
49 More than most
50 Unknown Jane
51 Bellini opera
53 Comic strip since 1932
58 Spill consequence
60 Clapping sea animal
61 It comes with string attached
62 Fighter's goal
63 "Legally Blonde" lead character
64 Without advantage or disadvantage
65 Display disdain, in a way
66 Large amount
67 Place for a clutch

DOWN

1 Assert without proof
2 Auto repair shop replacement car
3 Long, loose overcoat
4 Blokes
5 Not make the grade
6 Sicily's mountain
7 Soybean food
8 Farthest orbital point
9 Flight segment
10 Procure
11 Beach or ham
12 Inflated self-image
13 Just recruited
21 Change from commercial to residential, e.g.
22 "Rumor ___ it . . ."
26 Bath powder
27 Recess at church
30 "The Loco-Motion" singer, Little ___
31 "Go, team!"
32 Tributary of the Missouri River

33 It holds valuables
34 Olfactory organ
35 Well in the past
36 One of the three bears
37 Russian river or mountains
38 Turnpike structure
39 Stock value
40 A humorous play on words
44 "___ of Frankenstein"
45 Pokes fun at
46 Hit the big time

47 Strikes down, in the Bible
48 Inventor's document
50 Mel's sitcom place
52 Like the old bucket of song
54 Bring exasperation
55 Carter of "Gimme a Break!"
56 Chip's buddy
57 Put out the birthday candles
58 Blvd. crossers
59 Word with "foil" or "can"

UNDER THE BIG TOP

ACROSS

1 ___ the Hutt ("Return of the Jedi" character)
6 Source of fiber
10 Take a load off
14 Branch of basket-making
15 Get carried away?
16 "First Lady of Song" Fitzgerald
17 Well-balanced individual?
20 "Family" actress Thompson
21 "___ a Male War Bride" (Grant movie)
22 Horticultural requirements
23 USMC enlistees
25 JFK airport posting
26 Swinging star?
32 Big Apple parade sponsor
33 Soak in water, as flax
34 One of the Great Lakes
37 "___ before beauty"
38 Firms, as abs
42 Part of SASE (Abbr.)
43 Soft ball?
45 "___ Quixote"
46 Grammarian's concern
48 One who doesn't saddle up?
52 "My country" follower
53 "___ Lang Syne"
54 "The final frontier"
57 Shakespeare, for one
59 Watchful pair?
63 Circus attraction
66 Give off
67 Movie theater
68 Extremely light wood
69 Without
70 Overwhelm with humor
71 Eddie Haskell, to Beaver

DOWN

1 Scribbles (with "down")
2 Large continent
3 Dallas' nickname
4 Advice from Bobby McFerrin
5 ___ Deco
6 Window-shop
7 Kelly of morning TV
8 Juice drinks
9 Right from the factory
10 Let go
11 "A Shot in the Dark" actress Sommer
12 Yukon vehicle
13 Old salts
18 "Puttin' on the ___"
19 Italian wine town
24 Three-piece piece
25 A couple words to Brutus
26 Govt. agent
27 Bad thing to fly into
28 Sharp-tongued
29 Game site

30 Some scale notes
31 Tire pattern
35 Pulitzer winner for "Picnic"
36 At any time
39 Poetic tributes
40 San Francisco hill
41 Knit one, ___ two
44 They're loaded
47 Article supplement
49 French goose egg
50 Sewer worker of "The Honeymooners"
51 Bit of praise

54 "___ A Lady"
55 Sleek feline
56 Former dictator Idi
57 It may be posted or jumped
58 Kournikova formerly of tennis
60 Harvard rival
61 Last word of an ultimatum
62 Token punishment
64 IV amounts
65 TV network initials since 1926

HAVE FUN!

ACROSS

1 Peak in Sicily
5 Type of music or food
9 Very overweight
14 Leopold's co-conspirator
15 Bread with a pocket
16 Carbo-loading meal
17 Jordanian, most likely
18 Norway's king until 1991
19 Oft-used keyboard key
20 Beautician's advice for having fun?
23 Chi follower
24 ___ tai
25 Watchmaker's advice for having fun?
33 Skywalker portrayer
34 Where the heart is
35 Reject
36 "Night" author Wiesel
37 Said twice, it's a candy
38 Teen's affliction
39 Winnebagos, e.g.
40 Middle Eastern king deposed in 1964
42 Ski downhill
44 Bird watcher's advice for having fun?
47 Hoff's "The ___ of Pooh"
48 Chicken-king connector
49 Artist's advice for having fun
58 Character set for computers
59 Prefix for gram or logical
60 Met star, perhaps
61 Sculpture in St. Peter's Basilica
62 Claim on property
63 More than passed
64 Photographer Adams
65 Camera essential
66 "Citizen ___" (1941)

DOWN

1 Airline to Jerusalem
2 Moved at a good clip
3 Orderly
4 "Dear" advice-giver
5 Kind of support
6 Offshore sight
7 Bryce Canyon National Park location
8 Mauna Loa output
9 Surgeon's decision
10 Stagecoach robber
11 "___ perpetua" (Idaho's motto)
12 Crock-Pot concoction, perhaps
13 Merit
21 German carmaker Fritz von
22 Islamic leader
25 Share equally
26 Plain-living sect
27 Strive for superiority
28 "The Mary Tyler Moore Show" spin-off
29 One billion years, in geology
30 Bring upon oneself

31 Capital of Belarus
32 Former significant others
33 Bandleader Alpert
37 Believe, as a story
38 "So that's it!"
40 Having three dimensions
41 Words before "of gold"
42 Wild West watering holes
43 One way to get to the top?

45 When to see Nick?
46 Shiny fabric
49 Famous bear
50 Words of explanation, to a speller
51 Mouth-cooling treats
52 It could make you switch gears
53 Brickell or Adams
54 Bismarck's st.
55 Costa ___
56 With neither indebted to the other
57 Sunshine State county

IT'S ALL GOOD

ACROSS

1 Bronchial allergy
7 Texas ___ (oil)
10 Military no-show
14 Repelled a fly
15 Greek shipper Onassis, informally
16 French novelist Emile
17 Great!
19 Folksy Guthrie
20 Valleyspeak word
21 TV's Southfork Ranch locale
23 Floe is a component of it
27 Moved in a curved path
28 Off the mark, as a throw
29 Cute as a button
32 West End stagings
33 Form a secret merger?
34 Site of a famous boxing bite
35 Dry champagnes
36 Feeds the hogs
37 Legal start?
38 Rorschach's medium
39 Fleet of foot
40 Shipper's postings
41 Most indigent
43 Withdraw
44 Hindu queen (Var.)
45 Informal cafes
46 Fine-tune
48 Ancient people of Britain

49 Predecessor of Roger and Pierce
50 Great
56 Diplomat's asset
57 Misjudge
58 Tick away
59 Gets one's goat
60 Eligibility factor
61 Body on The Hill

DOWN

1 Braying beast
2 Moo ___ pork
3 Word with "spin" or "notch"
4 It'll unharden your garden
5 Small falcons
6 One with a pack-a-day habit
7 Sprinter's destination
8 Poetic preposition
9 Gets supplies to troops, in a way
10 Colorful shrub
11 Champion
12 Spanish pot
13 Neighbor of Myanmar
18 Island guitar, briefly
22 Farm land measure
23 Digestive enzyme
24 Francis of "What's My Line?"
25 Ace or snack food
26 Jay followers

Puzzle 95 by Alice Walker

27 One way to become a father
29 In the air
30 Town in many Westerns
31 Rubs out
33 "Fur ___" (Beethoven)
36 Climbing plant with fragrant flowers
37 Alliance basis, perhaps
39 Pride and envy, e.g.
40 What hairdressers do
42 Intimidates

43 Rags to ___
45 Pen name
46 Italian wine-producing city
47 First word in a diary
48 Take off the coat
51 Foot-pound subdivision
52 State bordering Colo.
53 Clean Air Act org.
54 Body shop fig.
55 Maiden name intro

TRY IT, YOU'LL LIKE IT

ACROSS
1 Dizzy Gillespie's music
6 Word with "bar" or "binary"
10 Little bits
14 Roll with the punches
15 Cutlass, for one
16 Heir to the Ponderosa
17 Try
19 Diving position
20 "Lilies of the Field" song
21 Japanese Prime Minister Hirobumi
22 "Its been ___ pleasure"
23 Try
27 Certain woodwind player
29 Obsessed with
30 Plays in city after city
31 Bust supporters
36 "___ the season to be jolly"
37 Buenos ___
38 Bud's funny bud
39 White-flowered shrubs
42 Fife player's percussion
44 Track-and-field contest
45 Cause to expand, as pupils
46 Try
51 007, e.g.
52 Guy who's all thumbs
53 Foot portion
56 Cape Town cash
57 And try again . . .

60 Lid irritation
61 Asia's shrinking sea
62 Smoothes, as the way
63 ___ over heels
64 Like an owl, supposedly
65 Mules, hinnies and such

DOWN
1 ___ 1,000 (get three hits in three at-bats)
2 Cheese from Holland
3 Where breads, cakes and pastries may be made
4 Outdoors, as a concert
5 "Harper Valley ___"
6 Raccoon relative
7 James of "The Andromeda Strain"
8 Outlawed pesticide
9 Suffix with Taiwan or Peking
10 Carrot's principal feeder
11 "Farewell" from France
12 Capital of Senegala
13 Small silvery fish
18 Pinball violation
22 Performs in a play
24 Naval monogram on many ships
25 "The Prince of ___" (1991)
26 ___, tens, hundreds, . . .

Puzzle 96 by Adrian Powell

27 "Beetle Bailey" dog
28 A way to cook eggs
31 Michelangelo work
32 Make a faux pas
33 Obstacle to success or large sea bird
34 Burglar's swag
35 Completely convinced
37 Middle East gulf
40 Changed for the better
41 Nice and tidy
42 Comedian Conway
43 Llama cousins

45 Resist with boldness
46 Swampland
47 Fine print, perhaps
48 Safari country
49 Old Roman wraps
50 "Knights of the Round ___" (1953)
54 Canadian Native American
55 Pianist Dame Myra
57 Like most fish in sushi
58 "Mentalist" Geller
59 Red or Dead body of water

GRAMMAR LESSON

ACROSS

1 Does a send-up
5 A way to get it down
8 Ricky to Lucy, "Honey, ___"
14 Tell, in detail
16 Moliere's trickster
17 "The Maltese Falcon" novelist
19 "Star Wars" royalty
20 Parliamentary vote
21 They may be deserted
22 Alphabet sequence
24 Biblical verb
26 Big advantages in sports
33 William Tell's canton
34 Legal thing
35 A load of gossip
36 Neutral color
37 Churchillian gesture
38 "Barbara ___" (Beach Boys tune)
39 "___ before beauty"
40 Place of perfection
42 "___ Yeller"
43 Piece of advice
44 Social Security check, e.g.
48 Notorious Barrow
49 "___ of Love" (1989)
50 It may seal the deal
53 Game animal
55 Development divisions
58 Results of imperialism
62 Kidnap
63 Like some stock
64 Precisely
65 Nickname for either of two AL teams
66 "Desperate Housewives" Hatcher

DOWN

1 Verb used in recipes
2 Sound from a chapel tower, perhaps
3 ___ quam videri
4 The Protestant Reformation, e.g.
5 "American ___" (1999 comedy)
6 In a competent way
7 Intelligently planned progress
8 "This ___ recording"
9 Hudson, on TV
10 It spins its wheels
11 Car manufacturer Fritz von
12 Wee arachnid
13 Tall Tolkien creatures
15 Gaucho's rope
18 Jessica, of the PTL Club scandal
23 Still in rehearsals
25 Matters to be voted upon
26 Prankster
27 Address an audience
28 Under full legal age
29 Gidget portrayer Sandra

Puzzle 97 by David Kahn

30 "___ worse than death"

31 Prepared to make a defensive stand

32 "George Washington ___ here"

37 Feature of many R-rated films

38 Swiss sight

41 Make a selection

42 Eyelike spot, as on peacock feathers

45 Brilliant thing that comes to mind

46 Pound sounds

47 Zedong follower

50 "Scram!"

51 Vagrant

52 "Betsy's Wedding" actor

54 Game of chance

56 "___ Colors" (Cyndi Lauper chart-topper)

57 Lifeline reader

59 Suffix with Israel

60 Tom of cowboy flicks

61 Bygone Reagan program, briefly

ODDER COUPLES

ACROSS

1 Infamous Colombian city
5 "Diff'rent Strokes" actress Plato
9 Bunk
14 "___ I say more?"
15 Dash
16 Downsizing, so to speak
17 ___ Roberts University
18 Went caroling
19 Snake hazard
20 Odd combo?
23 Chow down
24 Cause of a swelled head
25 Charged particle
26 Batter's achievement
29 Catch phrase
31 Outlawed pollutants in the U.S.
32 Place for a hammer
33 Franklin of soul
35 Scandinavian capital
36 Odd actor combo?
41 Soprano's big number
42 Determine the costs of
43 Airport shuttle vehicle, often
44 Informal eatery
46 Nuclear
50 Noted twin
51 M.D. provider
52 Jeanne d'Arc's title, briefly
53 Soccer phenom Freddy
54 Odd actor combo?
57 "Mrs. Miniver" star Garson
60 "___ Colors" (Cyndi Lauper chart-topper)
61 Direct
62 In conflict
63 Some U.S. inductees, once
64 Aquatic bird
65 Dorkish
66 Has an obligation
67 Basilica feature

DOWN

1 One hundred dollar bills, slangily
2 Common rooftop item, once
3 Crude shelter
4 Without urgency
5 Worked for HGTV
6 Site of a last stand
7 "Peter Pan" pooch
8 Church of England group
9 Sanctuaries
10 Bovine beasts
11 Flesh and blood
12 Spanish one
13 "The Wizard of Oz" studio
21 Moist-eyed
22 Wimbledon stroke

26 Musical silence
27 "Road to ___" (Hope-Crosby film)
28 Fairway pick
30 Mediterranean area
31 Stage
34 Doris Day classic
35 About
36 Comedian Chappelle
37 OPEC member
38 Pizazz
39 Like vegetarian dishes
40 Daisylike bloom

44 Kind of "tomato" or "bomb"
45 "What ___ doing?!"
47 End a squabble
48 Perfect examples
49 Go bad, like milk
52 Barbecue, for one
54 Unlike Charles Atlas
55 Attraction
56 Korbut, of gymnastic fame
57 One-liner
58 1-95, for one (Abbr.)
59 You homophone

ACROSS

1 When tripled, a WWII film
5 Large member of violin family
10 Underworld river
14 McGregor of "Trainspotting"
15 Provide with necessities
16 Hyde Park four-wheeler
17 "Feet first" and "No pushing"?
19 Russian spacecraft series
20 "___ Little Indians"
21 Lab bottles
22 Mining tools
23 Some salon workers
25 Supply funding for
26 Precisely (with "to")
27 Loggers' work sites
30 Muhammad's birthplace
33 Sound from the floor above
34 Time-wasting bother
35 Eunuch's charge
37 Man-mouse link
38 Affluent
41 ___ lazuli
43 Drifted off
44 Mountain transport
46 Handwoven rugs
47 Crayola color
51 Up to now
53 Nancy Drew creator
54 It may be pint-sized
55 Racetrack shape
56 Midafternoon to midnight stint
58 Suffix with "song" or "gab"
59 Trip the light fantastic
60 Where to find most people
61 Pretentious
62 Expresses impatience, in a way
63 Collision consequence

DOWN

1 They're held for questioning
2 Baby bird of prey
3 Day many save for
4 "___ away we go!"
5 Cherry shade
6 Make equal, uniform, corresponding or matching
7 Soothes
8 They may come in a pack
9 Rhea's Roman counterpart
10 Joins wires or film
11 Semi service station?
12 One way to extract a tooth
13 Yuletide, briefly
18 Andrew Lloyd Webber musical
22 Result of splitting hairs?
24 Fond du ___, Wisconsin
25 Bust opposite
27 Challenger
28 Garr of "Young Frankenstein"

Puzzle 99 by Hal Crosham

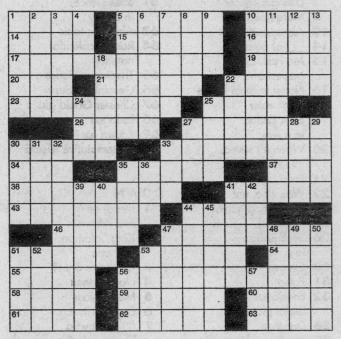

29 They may be filled with jets
30 Traps or yaps
31 Adam's garden
32 Not running, as clothes
33 Not to
35 Farming tools
36 Tack on
39 Good quality in a friend
40 Former Russian ruler
41 Features of footballs
42 Noah's craft
44 Type of warfare or coat

45 Eats or drinks too much
47 Peter Sellers film "___ There"
48 Cause for celebration, on the job
49 Like a sprite
50 Coup ___ (political rebellion)
51 Upholstered piece
52 No longer in love with
53 "The Bridge on the River ___"
56 Radical grp. of the '60s
57 Owned

HOLDING COURT

ACROSS

1 Dillinger chaser
5 More gelid
10 Abner cartoonist
14 ___ of passage
15 Mr. Hall, of gameshows
16 Nobel Institute locale
17 "No" voter
18 Seek justice, in a way
20 When it's saved, it's taken
21 Press agent?
22 Wax eloquent
23 The mating game?
25 "Macbeth" figures
26 Seek justice, in a way
30 On one's toes
31 Pallid
32 Enceladus' burial place
36 Disfigure
37 Puts into motion
41 Aspiration
42 Cuernavaca tip, perhaps
44 No longer fast
45 Therefore
47 Seek justice, in a way
51 Frolicked
54 Netherlands city (with "The")
55 Suburbs suburb
56 Blacken, as barbecue fare
58 Boat's bow
61 Seek justice, in a way
63 Almanac topic
64 Roman calendar notation
65 Theater audience
66 Geraint's spouse
67 Chester Gould girl
68 Lounged
69 Rooms for contemplative leisure

DOWN

1 Mardi or foie follower
2 King Solomon had one
3 Offensive ones?
4 Nor partner
5 Mischievous
6 English Lit, e.g.
7 "___ the wild blue yonder"
8 School near Slough
9 Stimpy's cartoon friend
10 Deteriorate
11 Like the gong's origin
12 Pass it in church
13 Walesa's countrymen
19 Of two minds
24 Suffix denoting female
25 Vaudeville dancer's "prop"

Puzzle 100 by Gayle Dean

26 Mash down
27 Cupid appendages
28 Belts, as a homer
29 Touching game
33 Type of mandarin orange
34 Affable
35 "Undecided" Brothers
38 Desideratum
39 Energy source
40 Carpet type
43 Crush the spirit
46 Blew, as a volcano

48 Singer McEntire
49 Daybed
50 Injured
51 Equip again
52 Word with "zinc" or "nitrous"
53 "Two ___ for Sister Sara"
56 Earth clump
57 Heist tally
59 Balder's dad
60 Becomes one with another
62 Greek letter

SOLUTIONS

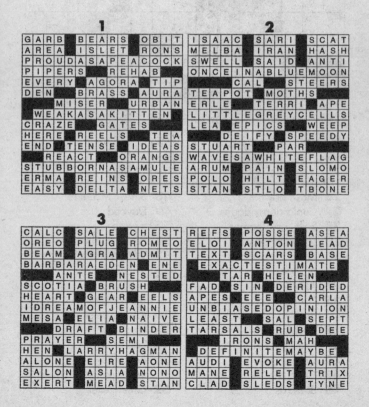

1

G	A	R	B		B	E	A	R	S		O	B	I	T
A	R	E	A		I	S	L	E	T		R	O	N	S
P	R	O	U	D	A	S	A	P	E	A	C	O	C	K
P	I	P	E	R	S			R	E	H	A	B		
E	V	E	R	Y		A	G	O	R	A		T	I	P
D	E	N			B	R	A	S	S		A	U	R	A
			M	I	S	E	R			U	R	B	A	N
W	E	A	K	A	S	A	K	I	T	T	E	N		
C	R	A	Z	E		G	A	T	E	S				
H	E	R	E		R	E	E	L	S			T	E	A
E	N	D		T	E	N	S	E		I	D	E	A	S
		R	E	A	C	T			O	R	A	N	G	S
S	T	U	B	B	O	R	N	A	S	A	M	U	L	E
E	R	M	A		R	E	I	N	S		O	R	E	S
E	A	S	Y		D	E	L	T	A		N	E	T	S

2

I	S	A	A	C		S	A	R	I		S	C	A	T
M	E	L	B	A		I	R	A	N		H	A	S	H
S	W	E	L	L		S	A	I	D		A	N	T	I
O	N	C	E	I	N	A	B	L	U	E	M	O	O	N
				C	A	L			S	T	E	E	R	S
T	E	A	P	O	T		M	O	T	H	S			
E	R	L	E			T	E	R	R	I		A	P	E
L	I	T	T	L	E	G	R	E	Y	C	E	L	L	S
L	E	A		E	P	I	C	S			W	E	E	P
		D	E	I	F	Y		S	P	E	E	D	Y	
S	T	U	A	R	T			P	A	R				
W	A	V	E	S	A	W	H	I	T	E	F	L	A	G
A	R	U	M		P	A	I	N			S	L	O	M	O
P	O	L	O		H	I	L	T			E	A	G	E	R
S	T	A	N		S	T	L	O			T	B	O	N	E

3

C	A	L	C		S	A	L	E		C	H	E	S	T
O	R	E	O		P	L	U	G		R	O	M	E	O
B	E	A	M		A	G	R	A		A	D	M	I	T
B	A	R	B	A	R	A	E	D	E	N		E	N	E
		A	N	T	E			N	E	S	T	E	D	
S	C	O	T	I	A		B	R	U	S	H			
H	E	A	R	T		G	E	A	R		E	E	L	S
I	D	R	E	A	M	O	F	J	E	A	N	N	I	E
M	E	S	A		E	L	I	A		N	A	I	V	E
		D	R	A	F	T		B	I	N	D	E	R	
P	R	A	Y	E	R		S	E	M	I				
H	E	N		L	A	R	R	Y	H	A	G	M	A	N
A	L	O	N	E		E	I	R	E		A	O	N	E
S	A	L	O	N		A	S	I	A		N	O	N	O
E	X	E	R	T		M	E	A	D		S	T	A	N

4

R	E	F	S		P	O	S	S	E		A	S	E	A
E	L	O	I		A	N	T	O	N		L	E	A	D
T	E	X	T		S	C	A	R	S		B	A	S	E
	E	X	A	C	T	E	S	T	I	M	A	T	E	
			T	A	R		H	E	L	E	N			
F	A	D		S	I	N		D	E	R	I	D	E	D
A	P	E	S		E	E	E			C	A	R	L	A
U	N	B	I	A	S	E	D	O	P	I	N	I	O	N
L	E	A	S	T			S	A	L			S	E	P	T
T	A	R	S	A	L	S		R	U	B		D	E	E
			I	R	O	N	S		M	A	H			
	D	E	F	I	N	I	T	E	M	A	Y	B	E	
A	U	D	I		E	V	O	K	E		A	U	R	A
M	A	N	E		R	E	L	E	T		T	R	I	X
C	L	A	D		S	L	E	D	S		T	Y	N	E

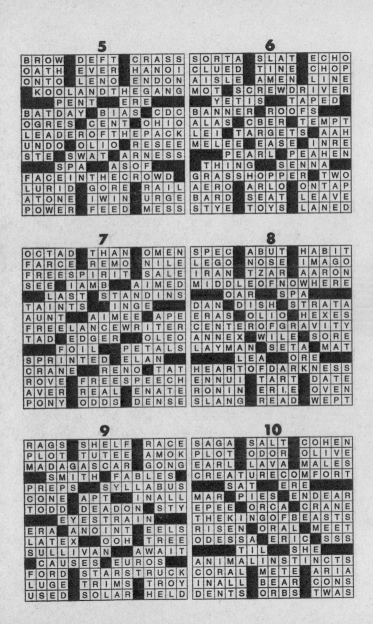

5

B	R	O	W		D	E	F	T		C	R	A	S	S
O	A	T	H		E	V	E	R		H	A	N	O	I
O	N	T	O		L	E	N	O		E	N	D	O	N
	K	O	O	L	A	N	D	T	H	E	G	A	N	G
			P	E	N	T			E	R	E			
B	A	T	D	A	Y		B	I	A	S		C	D	C
O	G	R	E	S		C	E	N	T		O	H	I	O
L	E	A	D	E	R	O	F	T	H	E	P	A	C	K
U	N	D	O		O	L	I	O		R	E	S	E	E
S	T	E		S	W	A	T		A	R	N	E	S	S
			S	P	A			A	S	O	F			
F	A	C	E	I	N	T	H	E	C	R	O	W	D	
L	U	R	I	D		G	O	R	E		R	A	I	L
A	T	O	N	E		I	W	I	N		U	R	G	E
P	O	W	E	R		F	E	E	D		M	E	S	S

6

S	O	R	T	A		S	L	A	T		E	C	H	O
C	L	U	E	D		T	I	N	E		C	H	O	P
A	I	S	L	E		A	M	E	N		L	I	N	E
M	O	T		S	C	R	E	W	D	R	I	V	E	R
			Y	E	T	I	S		T	A	P	E	D	
B	A	N	N	E	R		R	O	O	F	S			
A	L	A	S		C	B	E	R		T	E	M	P	T
L	E	I		T	A	R	G	E	T	S		A	A	H
M	E	L	E	E		E	A	S	E		I	N	R	E
			P	E	A	R	L		P	E	A	H	E	N
	T	H	I	N	G		S	E	N	N	A			
G	R	A	S	S	H	O	P	P	E	R		T	W	O
A	E	R	O		A	R	L	O		O	N	T	A	P
B	A	R	D		S	E	A	T		L	E	A	V	E
S	T	Y	E		T	O	Y	S		L	A	N	E	D

7

O	C	T	A	D		T	H	A	N		O	M	E	N
F	A	R	C	E		R	E	M	O		N	I	L	E
F	R	E	E	S	P	I	R	I	T		S	A	L	E
S	E	E		I	A	M	B		A	I	M	E	D	
			L	A	S	T		S	T	A	N	D	I	N	S
T	A	I	N	T	S		I	N	G	E				
A	U	N	T		A	I	M	E	E		A	P	E	
F	R	E	E	L	A	N	C	E	W	R	I	T	E	R
T	A	D		E	D	G	E	R		O	L	E	O	
			F	O	I	L		P	E	T	A	L	S	
S	P	R	I	N	T	E	D		E	L	A	N		
C	R	A	N	E		R	E	N	O		T	A	T	
R	O	V	E		F	R	E	E	S	P	E	E	C	H
A	V	E	R		R	E	A	L		E	N	A	T	E
P	O	N	Y		O	D	D	S		D	E	N	S	E

8

S	P	E	C		A	B	U	T		H	A	B	I	T
L	E	G	O		N	O	S	E		I	M	A	G	O
I	R	A	N		T	Z	A	R		A	A	R	O	N
M	I	D	D	L	E	O	F	N	O	W	H	E	R	E
			O	A	R			S	P	A				
D	A	N		D	I	S	H		S	T	R	A	T	A
E	R	A	S		O	L	I	O		H	E	X	E	S
C	E	N	T	E	R	O	F	G	R	A	V	I	T	Y
A	N	N	E	X		W	I	L	E		S	O	R	E
L	A	Y	M	A	N		S	E	T	A		M	A	T
				L	E	A			O	R	E			
H	E	A	R	T	O	F	D	A	R	K	N	E	S	S
E	N	N	U	I		T	A	R	T		D	A	T	E
R	O	N	I	N		E	R	I	E		O	V	E	N
S	L	A	N	G		R	E	A	D		W	E	P	T

9

R	A	G	S		S	H	E	L	F		R	A	C	E
P	L	O	T		T	U	T	E	E		A	M	O	K
M	A	D	A	G	A	S	C	A	R		G	O	N	G
			S	M	I	T	H		F	A	B	L	E	S
P	R	E	P	S		S	Y	L	L	A	B	U	S	
C	O	N	E		A	P	T		I	N	A	L	L	
T	O	D	D		D	E	A	D	O	N		S	T	Y
			E	Y	E	S	T	R	A	I	N			
E	R	A		A	N	O	I	N	T		E	E	L	S
L	A	T	E	X		O	O	H		T	R	E	E	
S	U	L	L	I	V	A	N		A	W	A	I	T	
			C	A	U	S	E	S		E	U	R	O	S
F	O	R	D		S	T	A	R	S	T	R	U	C	K
L	U	G	E		T	R	I	M	S		T	R	O	Y
U	S	E	D		S	O	L	A	R		H	E	L	D

10

S	A	G	A		S	A	L	T		C	O	H	E	N
P	L	O	T		O	D	O	R		O	L	I	V	E
E	A	R	L		L	A	V	A		M	A	L	E	S
C	R	E	A	T	U	R	E	C	O	M	F	O	R	T
			S	A	T			E	R	E				
M	A	R		P	I	E	S		E	N	D	E	A	R
E	P	E	E		O	R	C	A		C	R	A	N	E
T	H	E	K	I	N	G	O	F	B	E	A	S	T	S
R	I	S	E	N		O	R	A	L		M	E	E	T
O	D	E	S	S	A		E	R	I	C		S	S	S
				T	I	L			S	H	E			
A	N	I	M	A	L	I	N	S	T	I	N	C	T	S
C	O	R	A	L		M	E	T	E		A	R	I	A
I	N	A	L	L		B	E	A	R		C	O	N	S
D	E	N	T	S		O	R	B	S		T	W	A	S

11

S	A	Y	S	O		A	N	T	E		M	A	K	O
O	N	A	N	D		M	O	O	T		O	M	A	R
F	O	L	L	O	W	P	R	E	C	E	D	E	N	T
A	T	T		M	I	S	T		E	V	E	N	T	S
S	E	A	L	E	D		H	O	T	E	L			
		I	T	E	R		M	E	N		P	A	N	
B	O	M	B	E		O	D	E	R		T	O	N	E
O	B	E	Y	R	E	G	U	L	A	T	I	O	N	S
I	O	N	A		G	E	N	E		A	G	L	E	T
L	E	D		T	O	R		T	A	M	E			
			R	A	I	S	E		S	P	R	A	N	G
A	S	P	E	N	S		A	C	H	E		L	I	E
S	T	I	C	K	T	O	T	H	E	R	U	L	E	S
T	I	L	T		I	D	E	A		E	N	A	C	T
A	R	L	O		C	E	N	T		D	O	N	E	E

12

P	U	F	F		R	A	T	S			G	L	E	E
A	R	O	O		E	C	H	O		B	O	A	R	D
L	E	A	R		G	U	R	U		L	U	C	I	D
M	A	L	E	C	A	T	O	R	T	U	R	K	E	Y
			S	H	R	E	W		R	E	D			
B	A	B	I	E	D		I	S	I	S		B	R	A
O	M	E	G	A		S	N	O	B		B	E	E	N
R	I	G	H	T	T	O	T	H	E	P	O	I	N	T
E	D	I	T		H	I	H	O		A	N	N	A	S
D	E	N		S	I	T	E		S	N	U	G	L	Y
			F	O	E		T	H	U	D	S			
A	W	A	R	D	F	O	R	A	N	A	C	T	O	R
C	A	C	A	O		B	A	L	K		A	R	L	O
E	N	N	U	I		I	S	L	E		R	E	D	O
D	E	E	D		T	H	E	N		D	E	S	K	

13

R	A	N	U	P		T	Y	P	O		O	P	A	L
I	W	A	S	A		R	E	A	P		P	E	L	E
S	E	B	E	R	G	A	N	D	H	A	R	L	O	W
E	D	S		M	O	P		E	L	A	T	E	D	
			E	E	L		B	L	A	H				
G	A	S	P	S	F	O	R	A	I	R		A	B	E
U	T	I	C	A		N	O	R	A		S	L	E	D
S	A	L	O	N		B	Y	E		C	H	I	L	I
T	R	O	T		T	A	C	O		H	A	B	I	T
S	I	S		B	R	I	E	F	M	O	V	I	E	S
			R	A	I	L		E	K	E				
T	A	M	A	L	E		E	N	E		Z	O	O	
A	V	O	I	D	D	I	S	C	U	S	S	I	N	G
K	I	L	N		O	T	T	O		U	P	P	E	R
E	D	D	Y		N	O	U	N		P	A	S	S	E

14

E	D	N	A		A	P	R	O	N		R	A	T	A
K	E	E	L		N	A	I	V	E		U	P	O	N
E	M	A	I	L	A	T	T	A	C	H	M	E	N	T
S	O	R	B	I	C		A	L	T	O		X	Y	Z
			I	C	O	N		S	A	N	E			
L	O	N		K	N	E	E		R	E	D	E	Y	E
I	N	O	R		D	E	N	S		S	E	V	E	N
F	S	T	O	P	A	D	J	U	S	T	M	E	N	T
T	E	M	P	O		S	O	D	A		A	N	T	E
S	T	E	E	L	S		Y	A	L	E		T	A	R
			S	L	O	E		N	E	R	O			
T	I	S		O	U	R	S		S	I	T	S	A	T
G	S	T	R	I	N	G	P	U	R	C	H	A	S	E
I	L	I	A		D	O	U	S	E		E	V	E	R
F	E	R	N		S	T	R	A	P		R	E	A	M

15

T	A	B	O	R		M	A	C	E		A	N	N	E
S	C	O	P	E		I	D	O	L		S	O	U	R
A	N	T	E	S		N	O	P	A	R	K	I	N	G
R	E	T	R	E	A	D		S	T	E	A	R	N	S
			L	A	N	G		H	E	E	D			
U	N	E		T	O	R	E		D	O	W	S	E	S
N	U	N	S		R	E	I	N		S	E	P	I	A
A	B	E	L		A	N	N	U	M		B	E	D	S
P	I	C	O	T		T	O	B	E		B	E	E	S
T	A	K	E	R	S		U	S	D	A		D	R	Y
			I	T	I	S		I	N	C	L			
S	C	R	A	P	E	R		S	A	I	L	I	N	G
C	R	O	S	S	W	A	L	K		M	I	M	E	O
O	A	T	S		E	Q	U	I		A	N	I	S	E
T	M	E	N		D	I	G	S		L	E	T	T	S

16

S	C	A	M	P		P	I	P	E		S	H	E	S
I	L	L	E	R		O	V	A	L		L	O	S	T
P	I	L	L	O	W	T	A	L	K		U	R	S	A
S	P	Y		M	O	A	N		M	I	S	E	R	
			P	O	R	T		C	H	I	N	E	S	E
S	W	E	E	T	N	O	T	H	I	N	G	S		
O	R	A	T	E		E	A	S	E		H	I	T	
D	A	R	E		M	E	N	D	S		M	O	N	O
A	P	T		A	E	R	O		T	I	E	R	S	
		H	U	G	S	A	N	D	K	I	S	S	E	S
N	E	W	N	E	S	S		R	I	P	E			
A	M	O	L	E		H	A	L	T		C	R	Y	
S	I	R	E		G	O	O	G	O	O	E	Y	E	S
A	L	M	S		A	N	N	O		E	V	A	D	E
L	E	S	S		B	E	E	N		S	E	N	O	R

17

```
BETHS FEDS SCAN
OBOES RAIL ORLY
COLLEGETRY LAOS
ALLI OUST PASTE
  ASCEND BACH
  AXE SHAPEDUP
EAGLE AWARE ITO
GTO RACECAR EAR
ATL TWEAK BATHE
DAFFIEST WAD
  CLOD DOGMAS
ALLEN CLAW IRIS
ROUX MAINSTREET
ABBE AGED WEAVE
BESS DENY ASSET
```

18

```
TALL SOFAR CRIB
ILIA PRADO HIRE
LEAVEITTOBEAVER
ERASE SEALANE
  CLIP RELET
BOSCH TENANT
YOURE ALES COP
THETWILIGHTZONE
EST MICA RECUR
  HEPCAT YEAST
SQUID NETS
AUNTIES ATILT
FATHERKNOWSBEST
ERIE LINEN IVAN
STER EMERY DIRT
```

19

```
PECS EWERS OWL
UPON LILACS RAY
SECONDSIGHT FIR
SEAWEED SNIFFLE
  CAROM ALE
SPAT MINUTEMAN
REAPER LIZ TALE
ATL NEEDLER NEO
STAB PRE REBORN
HOURGLASS CART
  ELY TUDOR
READAPT LOURDES
ODE DAYGLOPAINT
MIR SIPPER GETA
ATO DEANS ETON
```

20

```
SARA PASTA HOST
ALAS ISLAM ELLE
KISSMEKATE ALIT
SEPIA VALIDATE
  GNUS INA
MANOFLAMANCHA
TAT ROOMY SHALE
ALAR SPORT EVES
RELIT PRIOR OPT
SEVENYEARITCH
  ELI DELI
NESTEGGS EPEES
ALAI HELLODOLLY
DAMN TRIER FLAN
ALEG SEDER FANE
```

21

```
PHILS BASS HOST
EATUP ALOT INKY
TAILORMADE NEAP
ASSURE RAINDATE
  SANS SNARLED
SRO DEWS EPA
CAPRI ATOM NAYS
AZTEC MAN SCOOP
MESA SIFT KENYA
  RAE FACE EON
AWARDED PALS
MOLASSES REPAST
IRON AFTERTASTE
SMUG WOOL OCEAN
HYDE SEWS NEARS
```

22

```
USPS ALAS COAST
GLUT LENO OLLIE
HOMEOFSTRAYDOGS
STARS ZERO TNT
  NICE ACT
CAT EZRATHEPOET
AMYGRANT SABER
LOPE RELAY PILE
EVENS ACETATES
BEATHARSHLY SRS
  AXE ELLS
ADD KIDS ETUIS
BRITISHCURRENCY
CANOE OOZE ATON
STEER TWIN DONE
```

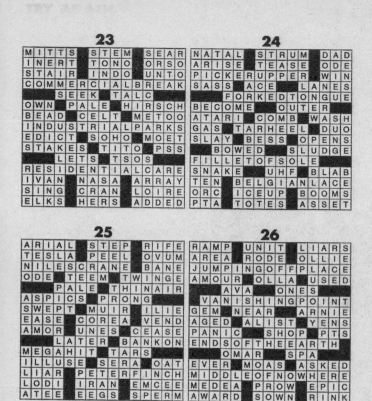

23

M	I	T	T	S		S	T	E	M		S	E	A	R
I	N	E	R	T		T	O	N	O		O	R	S	O
S	T	A	I	R		I	N	D	O		U	N	T	O
C	O	M	M	E	R	C	I	A	L	B	R	E	A	K
			S	E	E	K			T	A	L	C		
O	W	N		P	A	L	E		H	I	R	S	C	H
B	E	A	D		C	E	L	T		M	E	T	O	O
I	N	D	U	S	T	R	I	A	L	P	A	R	K	S
E	D	I	C	T		S	O	H	O		M	O	E	T
S	T	A	K	E	S		T	I	T	O		P	S	S
			L	E	T	S		T	S	O	S			
R	E	S	I	D	E	N	T	I	A	L	C	A	R	E
I	V	A	N		N	A	S	A		A	R	R	A	Y
S	I	N	G		C	R	A	N		L	O	I	R	E
E	L	K	S		H	E	R	S		A	D	D	E	D

24

N	A	T	A	L		S	T	R	U	M		D	A	D
A	R	I	S	E		T	E	A	S	E		O	D	E
P	I	C	K	E	R	U	P	P	E	R		W	I	N
S	A	S	S		A	C	E			L	A	N	E	S
			F	O	R	K	E	D	T	O	N	G	U	E
B	E	C	O	M	E			O	U	T	E	R		
A	T	A	R	I		C	O	M	B		W	A	S	H
G	A	S		T	A	R	H	E	E	L		D	U	O
S	L	A	Y		B	E	S	S		O	P	E	N	S
			B	O	W	E	D			S	L	U	D	G	E
F	I	L	L	E	T	O	F	S	O	L	E			
S	N	A	K	E			U	H	F		B	L	A	B
T	E	N		B	E	L	G	I	A	N	L	A	C	E
O	R	C		I	C	E	U	P			B	O	O	M	S
P	T	A		T	O	T	E	S		A	S	S	E	T

25

A	R	I	A	L		S	T	E	P		R	I	F	E
T	E	S	L	A		P	E	E	L		O	V	U	M
N	I	L	E	S	C	R	A	N	E		B	A	N	E
O	D	E		T	E	E	M		T	W	I	N	G	E
			P	A	L	E		T	H	I	N	A	I	R
A	S	P	I	C	S		P	R	O	N	G			
S	W	E	P	T		M	U	I	R		I	L	I	E
E	A	S	E		C	O	R	E	A		V	E	N	D
A	M	O	R		U	N	E	S		C	E	A	S	E
			L	A	T	E	R		B	A	N	K	O	N
M	E	G	A	H	I	T		T	A	R	S			
I	L	L	U	S	E		S	E	R	A		O	A	T
L	I	A	R		P	E	T	E	R	F	I	N	C	H
L	O	D	I		I	R	A	N		E	M	C	E	E
A	T	E	E		E	E	G	S		S	P	E	R	M

26

R	A	M	P		U	N	I	T		L	I	A	R	S
A	R	E	A		R	O	D	E		O	L	L	I	E
J	U	M	P	I	N	G	O	F	F	P	L	A	C	E
A	M	O	U	R		O	L	L	A		U	S	E	D
			A	V	A			O	N	E	S			
V	A	N	I	S	H	I	N	G	P	O	I	N	T	
G	E	M		N	E	A	R			A	R	N	I	E
A	G	E	D		A	L	I	S	T		Y	E	N	S
P	A	N	I	C			S	H	O	P		P	T	S
E	N	D	S	O	F	T	H	E	E	A	R	T	H	
			O	M	A	R			S	P	A			
E	V	E	R		M	O	A	S		A	S	K	E	D
M	I	D	D	L	E	O	F	N	O	W	H	E	R	E
M	E	D	E	A		P	R	O	W		E	P	I	C
A	W	A	R	D		S	O	W	N		R	I	N	K

27

N	O	S	H		F	I	G	S		B	A	C	C	A
A	N	T	I		U	T	A	H		U	N	A	R	M
I	C	E	D		C	O	V	E	R	I	N	G	U	P
F	E	T	I	S	H		E	L	U	L		E	D	S
			N	A	S	A		F	E	D	S			
S	H	A	G	G	I	N	G		R	E	M	O	T	E
C	A	R	P		A	I	R	S		R	O	B	E	S
R	I	L	L		S	T	U	P	E		K	E	N	T
A	T	E	A	M		A	M	E	N		E	A	S	E
M	I	N	C	E	D		P	A	R	I	S	H	E	S
			E	M	I	R		R	O	T	C			
Y	E	A		B	E	E	P		L	A	R	G	E	R
M	A	S	K	E	D	B	A	L	L		E	L	L	E
C	R	I	E	R		A	L	O	E		E	E	L	S
A	L	A	N	S		R	O	S	E		N	E	S	T

28

M	E	L	L	O		C	L	O	T		A	V	O	W
G	R	E	A	T		H	O	B	O		R	A	G	E
R	I	N	G	B	E	A	R	E	R		I	L	L	E
S	N	A	G		T	R	E	Y		C	O	P	E	D
			A	D	O				R	O	S	A	R	Y
M	A	T	R	O	N	O	F	H	O	N	O	R		
E	R	O	D	E		B	E	E	T	S		A	L	P
G	E	L	S		B	E	L	L	E		T	I	E	R
S	A	L		L	I	S	L	E		P	A	S	T	A
			B	R	I	D	E	A	N	D	G	R	O	O	M
G	R	O	U	S	E			O	A	R				
R	O	O	S	T		E	L	A	N		A	P	E	S
O	U	T	S		F	L	O	W	E	R	G	I	R	L
A	S	H	E		A	S	I	A		I	O	N	I	A
N	E	S	T		D	E	N	Y		O	N	S	E	T

29

P	A	A	R		A	N	T	I		R	A	B	B	I
E	R	S	E		L	E	A	H		O	R	L	O	N
L	E	A	V	E	F	O	R	A	M	O	M	E	N	T
T	A	P	E	D			A	D	A	M		W	O	O
			A	G	A	R		T	A	I	L			
R	E	P	L	A	C	E	S	O	M	E	O	N	E	
O	N	A		R	E	N	T			S	P	I	K	E
A	D	I	T		S	O	A	P	S		E	X	I	T
D	O	S	E	D		S	L	A	P		O	N	T	
	F	A	C	E	A	C	H	A	L	L	E	N	G	E
			H	A	L	O		N	E	A	R			
P	G	A		R	A	N	I			C	R	E	S	T
R	E	S	I	G	N	A	S	A	L	E	A	D	E	R
O	N	E	N	O		I	L	I	A		T	I	R	E
S	T	A	N	D		R	E	L	Y		A	T	E	E

30

S	L	E	D		A	L	I	T		A	R	D	O	R
T	A	R	O		T	A	R	A		F	A	U	N	A
A	S	A	M	A	T	T	E	R	O	F	F	A	C	T
T	I	S		M	I	E	N		T	I	T	L	E	S
S	K	E	W	E	R		E	V	E	R	S			
			O	N	E	S		E	L	M		G	A	P
S	C	R	O	D		E	A	R	L		A	N	N	A
N	O	I	F	S	A	N	D	S	O	R	B	U	T	S
U	R	N	S		M	A	D	E		O	N	S	E	T
B	E	G		S	A	T		D	A	D	E			
			D	O	Z	E	R		R	E	R	E	A	D
D	E	L	A	N	O		I	C	O	N		N	E	E
O	P	E	N	A	N	D	S	H	U	T	C	A	S	E
R	E	A	C	T		U	K	E	S		A	T	O	M
M	E	D	E	A		E	Y	R	E		P	E	P	S

31

A	T	M	S		E	G	O	S		E	C	L	A	T
B	R	I	M		D	O	R	Y		T	R	A	C	E
D	I	M	E	N	O	V	E	L		C	O	I	N	S
U	T	I	L	E		T	O	P	S	E	C	R	E	T
L	E	S	T	A	T			H	U	T				
			R	I	B	S		B	E	C	A	L	M	
S	A	D	E		L	O	O	N		R	O	G	U	E
Q	U	A	R	T	E	R	F	I	N	A	L	I	S	T
F	R	I	A	R		N	A	N	A		A	N	T	E
T	A	S	S	E	L		R	A	S	P				
			A	I	R			L	L	A	M	A	S	
P	O	G	O	S	T	I	C	K		A	G	E	N	T
S	T	E	N	O		P	E	N	N	Y	L	A	N	E
S	T	A	I	N		U	L	E	E		E	R	I	E
T	O	R	T	S		P	L	E	A		T	A	E	L

32

B	A	A	S		S	P	A	D	E		T	A	L	L
O	U	T	A		A	L	I	E	N		O	L	E	O
A	T	T	N		N	O	D	E	S		M	A	S	C
R	O	A	D	S	I	D	E	R	U	B	B	I	S	H
			S	A	T			E	E	L				
S	I	R		M	A	L	L		D	E	N	I	R	O
A	G	E	R		R	E	O	S		E	I	D	E	R
F	A	M	I	L	Y	O	F	P	U	P	P	I	E	S
E	V	I	T	A		S	T	A	N		S	O	S	O
R	E	T	A	R	D		S	N	I	P		T	E	N
			V	E	E			V	I	A				
C	A	N	V	A	S	S	T	R	E	T	C	H	E	R
R	I	C	E		E	T	H	E	R		M	E	R	E
A	D	O	S		R	E	E	D	S		E	R	I	N
M	A	S	T		T	E	N	S	E		S	E	C	T

33

A	R	C	H		S	H	O	D		S	C	A	B	
C	O	L	A		S	A	U	T	E		L	O	R	E
M	O	O	D		T	I	E	B	R	E	A	K	E	R
E	M	U		L	A	D	D		R	A	V	I	N	E
		D	E	I	G	N		A	I	R		E	A	T
C	O	N	V	E	Y	O	R	B	E	L	T			
A	L	I	E	N			H	E	R		U	C	L	A
P	E	N	N		D	I	O	D	E		L	A	O	S
E	O	E	S		R	O	D			M	A	N	E	T
			O	B	I	W	A	N	K	E	N	O	B	I
A	S	H		O	V	A		O	A	T	E	N		
S	N	O	O	Z	E		N	O	S	E		I	O	N
W	I	N	D	O	W	S	A	S	H		E	Z	R	A
A	P	E	D		A	T	S	E	A		L	E	A	P
N	E	S	S		Y	E	A	S			I	D	L	E

34

P	A	D		S	P	L	I	T		A	L	O	H	A
A	C	E		A	R	E	N	A		C	O	P	E	D
S	A	F	E	T	Y	I	N	N	U	M	B	E	R	S
S	C	O	N	E				G	R	E	E	N		
B	I	R	D		M	A	S	O	N	S		F	O	R
Y	A	M		P	A	N	T	S			B	I	T	E
			A	O	R	T	A		A	C	A	R	I	D
M	A	J	O	R	I	T	Y	R	U	L	E	S		
C	A	N	A	R	Y			I	A	M	B	I		
A	G	A	R		B	O	L	E	S			A	T	M
N	I	L		S	E	I	N	E	D		O	G	R	E
			Y	E	L	L	S			U	V	E	A	S
C	A	S	T	O	F	T	H	O	U	S	A	N	D	S
O	N	T	A	P		R	O	U	T	E		D	E	E
T	A	S	S	E		O	T	T	E	R		A	D	D

35

S	P	C	A		S	O	A	R	S			S	T	E
H	E	A	T		I	G	L	O	O		S	K	I	N
A	R	L	O		G	R	A	N	D	S	T	A	N	D
Q	U	I	N	I	N	E	S			I	O	T	A	S
			E	R	A	S		S	P	E	W			
P	R	I	M	A	L		A	L	A	R		S	S	N
E	A	V	E			F	R	A	G	R	A	N	C	E
S	T	A	N	D	A	R	D	B	E	A	R	E	R	S
C	O	N	T	I	N	U	E	S			M	E	A	T
I	N	A		A	K	I	N		A	L	A	R	M	S
			S	L	A	T		D	I	E	D			
I	S	S	U	E			M	E	E	T	I	N	G	S
S	T	A	N	D	S	T	I	L	L		L	O	L	A
L	I	N	G		E	A	S	E	L		L	A	O	S
E	R	E			C	R	E	D	O		O	H	M	S

36

C	L	A	S	P		S	H	A	D	Y		G	I	L
A	R	I	P	E		H	A	G	U	E		E	V	A
G	O	T	O	T	H	E	D	O	G	S		T	A	B
E	N	S	U	R	E		E	G	O		E	T	N	A
			S	O	A	P	S			U	T	A	H	A	N...

41

C	R	A	B		C	A	R	E		I	S	L	A	M
R	A	G	U		A	L	A	N		S	T	O	R	E
A	R	A	C	H	N	O	I	D		R	E	V	E	L
P	A	R	K	A	V	E	N	U	E		R	E	A	D
			A	R	A			Y	E	L	L	E	R	
L	O	W	R	I	S	K		K	I	O	S	K	S	
I	S	A	O		S	E	T	T	E	E		L	U	C
B	O	L	O	S		Y	E	A		S	H	A	D	E
E	L	L		A	N	S	E	L	M		I	N	O	N
L	E	S	L	I	E		L	O	N	G	E	S	T	
			T	O	L	E	D	O		N	O	H		
H	O	R	A		R	O	D	E	O	D	R	I	V	E
O	N	E	N	D		P	E	R	C	E	I	V	E	S
E	M	E	E	R		E	T	A	L		S	A	N	S
R	E	T	R	Y		D	O	S	E		E	N	T	O

42

A	S	O	F		M	O	N	T	E		F	A	C	T
D	A	N	O		E	P	E	E	S		E	T	U	I
A	G	E	R		R	E	A	C	T		M	O	T	E
M	O	O	G	S	Y	N	T	H	E	S	I	Z	E	R
			O	W	L	S			E	O	N			
D	I	C	T	A		E	B	B		P	I	P	E	S
O	F	A		M	O	S	A	I	C		S	O	L	O
O	N	C	E	I	N	A	B	L	U	E	M	O	O	N
M	O	A	N		O	M	E	L	E	T		C	P	A
S	T	O	O	D		E	L	O		U	S	H	E	R
			R	U	M			F	A	D	E			
T	H	E	M	O	O	R	O	F	V	E	N	I	C	E
W	A	D	I		L	A	N	A	I		I	D	O	L
A	U	N	T		A	N	T	R	A		O	L	L	A
S	L	A	Y		R	A	V	E	N		R	Y	A	N

43

A	L	E	S		P	E	R	K	S		S	E	E	M
D	E	V	O		S	T	I	N	T		I	R	M	A
Z	I	O	N		S	A	V	O	R		G	R	E	G
			L	I	T	T	L	E	B	I	G	H	O	R	N
T	R	U	C	E		S	P	A		R	Y	A		
H	E	T		X	M	E	N		S	U	B			
U	N	I	T		A	L	A	S		N	O	R	S	E
G	E	O	R	G	E	A	R	M	S	T	R	O	N	G
S	E	N	O	R		N	E	E	R		E	L	I	A
			T	O	O		S	W	I	M		E	D	D
A	M	A		S	U	P			C	A	P	E	S	
L	A	S	T	S	T	A	N	D	H	I	L	L		
L	O	P	E		S	N	A	R	E		T	A	R	A
A	R	I	A		E	D	G	A	R		E	Y	E	S
N	I	C	K		T	A	S	T	E		R	S	V	P

44

N	I	P		O	S	C	A	R		F	E	T	A	L
I	N	E		S	T	O	R	E		O	X	I	D	E
E	A	R		A	I	T	C	H		N	I	S	A	N
K	N	U	C	K	L	E	H	E	A	D	S			
R	E	S	E	A	L			A	N	A	T	O	M	Y
O	R	E	L		N	A	S	T	Y			M	I	D
			E	B	E	R	T			S	T	E	M	S
	E	L	B	O	W	M	A	C	A	R	O	N	I	
P	R	E	S	S			K	I	L	O	S			
A	M	O		G	R	E	T	A			S	A	S	E
M	A	N	A	T	E	E			N	A	U	S	E	A
			K	N	E	E	S	L	A	P	P	I	N	G
R	E	T	R	O		V	I	O	L	S		M	O	L
E	L	I	O	T		E	L	U	D	E		O	R	E
D	O	N	N	E		S	O	D	A	S		V	A	T

45

A	T	M	S		I	R	K	E	D		S	P	E	D
R	H	E	A		T	H	E	R	E		P	L	I	E
M	O	O	N	S	H	I	N	E	R		R	A	R	E
S	U	R	G	E	O	N	S		O	P	I	N	E	D
			U	N	T	O		A	G	A	T	E		
	A	S	I	S		S	A	R	A	N		T	A	D
P	R	U	N	E	R		L	I	T	E		A	C	E
R	E	N	E		E	V	A	D	E		C	R	I	B
E	N	G		A	H	E	M		D	R	O	I	D	S
P	A	L		P	E	R	O	N		O	D	A	Y	
			A	S	S	A	Y		A	T	O	P		
P	O	S	T	E	R		P	R	E	M	I	E	R	E
A	L	S	O		S	T	A	R	R	Y	E	Y	E	D
T	I	E	R		A	K	R	O	N		C	R	A	G
H	O	S	E		L	O	E	W	S		E	E	L	Y

46

C	A	R	P	E		W	A	S	P		S	I	R	E
A	N	A	I	S		A	L	A	R		A	V	I	D
F	A	C	E	T	O	F	A	C	E		T	A	N	G
E	S	E		A	V	E	S		S	P	U	N	K	Y
			C	A	T	E	R		P	U	R	R		
S	C	O	R	E	R		A	R	M	I	N	A	R	M
T	A	U	T		T	O	R	I	E	S		D	I	E
O	G	R	E	S		K	I	D		S	T	U	N	T
R	E	S		P	H	A	S	E	S		E	L	S	E
E	Y	E	T	O	E	Y	E		W	A	N	T	E	D
			E	R	A	S		H	A	R	T	E		
B	A	L	L	E	T		S	A	M	E		R	I	O
O	V	A	L		H	A	N	D	I	N	H	A	N	D
N	O	N	E		E	R	I	E		A	S	T	R	O
E	W	E	R		R	A	P	S		S	T	E	E	R

47

```
S C A D   A B B A S   U S D A
A R E A   I R I S H   G O A L
W O R K S L I K E A C H A R M
S P O O L   L E A S H   P E A
      T O L L S   T I A
T O M A T O     D A L L A S
U Z I   N O T E   D I D O S
T O T H E G R I N D S T O N E
U N T I L   S O S O   P I T
E S K I M O     S K E T C H
      E X O   T H E I R
A G O   I N T R O   E N T R Y
L A B O R T H E O B V I O U S
A L O E   H A S T A   E R L E
N E E R   S I S S Y   S E E R
```

48

```
S H O T   R O B E S   S P A T
L A V A   E A R T H   H U L A
O R A L   A R E N A   I T E M
W E L C O M E W A G O N
            R E D   R E B I D
H O T A I R   S T E E R A G E
A L A M O   B L O C     A N N
B I G I N T R O D U C T I O N
I V E   A U T O   H E N R I
T I N S M I T H   G A N G E S
S A D I E       P A N
      G R E E T I N G C A R D
E L A N   D A R E D   R O A R
G A L A   G R A C E   O N T O
O P A L   E L M E R   P E E P
```

49

```
T A P I R   A I R Y   T O P S
I N U R E   E R I E   O H I O
T E L E V I S I O N S T A N D
O W L   E R O S     K O R E A
      S C R A P   A B E   A D S
S C O R E S   G N A T S
N O V A   H I G H C H A I R
O M E N S   A L L   H E N R I
W O R K T A B L E   A N O N
      Y A X I S   S T R O N G
M B A   T E T   H O R S Y
A L I B I   H I F I   A H S
M E D I C I N E C A B I N E T
B E E T   L E A K   A C C R A
A P S E   L A P S   L E E R Y
```

50

```
A B I E   M E T R O   M O R E
M A N X   A V I O N   E D I T
O N K P   L O R R E   D O N E
K E Y O N A K E Y B O A R D
      R O D E       Y U L
L A S T L Y   T H O R   G E L
O C T E T   T H I N   C O L A
W H E R E T H E H E A R T I S
L E E S   E U R O   R O U T E
Y S L   C E D E   V E S P E R
      A B S       E O N S
P I T C H E R S T A R G E T
L O C O   O R A T E   O O P S
I N O N   T I G E R   A R E A
T Y N E   S E E R S   D E E R
```

51

```
A L C O A   E F T S   P A P A
N O H O W   N O E L   I R A N
S T E P L I V E L Y   C E N T
E S E   D O S E   S K A T E
L A R G E L Y   T H O U
      E W E   C H I P P E W A
A D D T O   K O O K   S L A P
Q U I C K E N O N E S P A C E
U S E R   T E E S   T E N O R
A T T A I N E D   C U E
      C R A B   S A N D M A N
S M O K E   R O W S   A N A
T A X I   M A K E T R A C K S
O M E N   A C R E   E X A L T
P A N G   P E A T   D E W E Y
```

52

```
S I R   D E L E S   D E M I T
A C E   E L A T E   I N O N E
C I R C L E T H E W A G O N S
H E A R   C E E   A M I D S T
A R N E T T   R A Y O N
      O R S O   U N N E R V E
C H I L I   P A L E D   Y E A
H O S E A   P I A   B E E R S
A L I   N A O M I   A S S A Y
D E S I G N S   T A C T
      T U N E S   S K E T C H
R E S A L E   A C T   E R L E
E A T S A S Q U A R E M E A L
B R A C T   E C L A T   A R E
A L G A E   D E L L S   T E N
```

53

```
S C A M   A W A K E   A S T I
T U F T   R O B I N   P E R M
A R T S   C O U N T S H E E P
P I E   M A L T   R A I S E S
H O R N I N   S P E N D
  M A R E S   O A K   H E M
S L A N T   T A R T   M A L I
C A T C H F O R T Y W I N K S
A C H Y   L O K I   A N D E S
R E S   B A G   A S H E S
  M A T E S   N O D O F F
A S S I S T   C I A O   M O O
H I T T H E S A C K   H E R A
A L O E   R U P E E   A L U M
B O W S   S E E D S   G Y M S
```

54

```
D I A S   A D E P T   B L O B
E R L E   M E D E A   L O S E
W A T E R I N G T R O U G H S
  N O S E   A Y E   M E S A S
    S A H L   R B I S
B A T T L E I T O U T   P A C
O N R A M P   H S T   P E E L
O D O R S   T I E   M E D I A
Z E U S   W E E   S O R R O W
E S T   H A L F S E R I O U S
    T O R E   T A T S
A L I A S   V I A   A C H E
G A T H E R I N G C L O U D S
O R E O   A S N E R   P R E P
G A M E   M E S S Y   E T N A
```

55

```
S L O T   T E A M   M C C O Y
P E P O   O G R E   A L I V E
A H E M   W A R N   I O T A S
C A R B O N D A T I N G
E R A S E   S A R I   R E C
  T R A Y   L E D   A N A
A F R O   M O R N   E A T E R
G O I N G O U T O N A L I M B
G A V E L   B E T E   T O Y S
I L E   O R E   E A S E
E S T   V A T S   A R E N A
  S E E I N G E Y E D O G
A D L I B   C O R N   G I L L
C R E D O   A R I D   O C T O
E S S E X   N E T S   S T E W
```

56

```
G A M   R I S K S   F L I N T
O L A   E T H I C   R O D E O
A O K   S O I L E R O S I O N
T H E S E   P O N E S
S A M U E L   S E A T L E S S
  U N D U E   I M I T A T E
F E D S   L A O   E R R O R
L A P   T U R F W A R   T N T
U R I A H   F E Y   T H E A
E L E G I E S   B E D I M
D E S E R T E D   S E N O R A
    S C R I P   P A V E R
H I T S T H E D I R T   E V E
A L A T E   N I N T H   R U N
L L O Y D   E T T E S   S E A
```

57

```
A T M E   C H A R D   J O L T
C R A M   H O M E R   O H I O
T O U C H E S O N E S T O E S
A D I E U   T I D A L   H U H
    E R G     R U G
R U N S O N E S E Y E O V E R
I T O   N A V A L   S T E L E
N I T A   T E R A S   A R I L
S C I F I   R A T E D   S H E
E A T O N E S H E A R T O U T
  R I D     S A E
O D E   G E T A T   I D A H O
W A S H O N E S H A N D S O F
E S A U   I C I E R   E T U I
S H I M   C H A N T   D A R T
```

58

```
B R A S   S T E P   A B A B A
B O R E   H E R O   C A S E S
C A T E   R A I L   T R E A T
D E N V E R C O L O R A D O
    E D S     O R E
A N G E R S   B O G   L A W S
S O A R S   A R R O W   L A P
S T P A U L M I N N E S O T A
E R E   S E E N O   T U N E R
T E S T   A N Y   S T E E R S
  R E S     S H E
A T L A N T A G E O R G I A
R O U N D   D E A R   O D D S
F O R C E   A N T E   R O D E
S T E E D   M E S S   E L S E
```

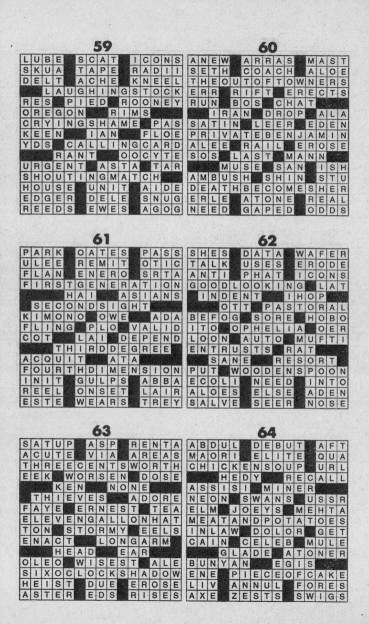

59

L	U	B	E		S	C	A	T			I	C	O	N	S
S	K	U	A		T	A	P	E			R	A	D	I	I
D	E	L	T		A	C	H	E		K	N	E	E	L	
	L	A	U	G	H	I	N	G	S	T	O	C	K		
R	E	S		P	I	E	D		R	O	O	N	E	Y	
O	R	E	G	O	N			R	I	M	S				
C	R	Y	I	N	G	S	H	A	M	E		P	A	S	
K	E	E	N			I	A	N			F	L	O	E	
Y	D	S		C	A	L	L	I	N	G	C	A	R	D	
			R	A	N	T			O	O	C	Y	T	E	
U	R	G	E	N	T		A	S	T	A		T	A	R	
S	H	O	U	T	I	N	G	M	A	T	C	H			
H	O	U	S	E		U	N	I	T		A	I	D	E	
E	D	G	E	R		D	E	L	E		S	N	U	G	
R	E	E	D	S		E	W	E	S		A	G	O	G	

60

A	N	E	W		A	R	R	A	S		M	A	S	T
S	E	T	H		C	O	A	C	H		A	L	O	E
T	H	E	O	U	T	O	F	T	O	W	N	E	R	S
E	R	R		R	I	F	T		E	R	E	C	T	S
R	U	N		B	O	S		C	H	A	T			
		I	R	A	N		D	R	O	P		A	L	A
S	A	T	I	N		L	E	E	R		E	D	E	N
P	R	I	V	A	T	E	B	E	N	J	A	M	I	N
A	L	E	E		R	A	I	L		E	R	O	S	E
S	O	S		L	A	S	T		M	A	N	N		
			M	U	S	E		S	A	N		I	S	H
A	M	B	U	S	H		S	H	I	N		S	T	U
D	E	A	T	H	B	E	C	O	M	E	S	H	E	R
E	R	L	E		A	T	O	N	E		R	E	A	L
N	E	E	D		G	A	P	E	D		O	D	D	S

61

P	A	R	K		O	A	T	E	S		P	A	S	S
U	L	E	E		R	E	M	I	T		O	T	I	C
F	L	A	N		E	N	E	R	O		S	R	T	A
F	I	R	S	T	G	E	N	E	R	A	T	I	O	N
			H	A	I			A	S	I	A	N	S	
	S	E	C	O	N	D	S	I	G	H	T			
K	I	M	O	N	O		O	W	E			A	D	A
F	L	I	N	G		P	L	O		V	A	L	I	D
C	O	T		L	A	I		D	E	P	E	N	D	
		T	H	I	R	D	D	E	G	R	E	E		
A	C	Q	U	I	T		A	T	A					
F	O	U	R	T	H	D	I	M	E	N	S	I	O	N
I	N	I	T		G	U	L	P	S		A	B	B	A
R	E	E	L		O	N	S	E	T		L	A	I	R
E	S	T	E		W	E	A	R	S		T	R	E	Y

62

S	H	E	S		D	A	T	A		W	A	F	E	R
T	A	L	K		U	S	E	S		E	R	O	D	E
A	N	T	I		P	H	A	T		I	C	O	N	S
G	O	O	D	L	O	O	K	I	N	G		L	A	T
			I	N	D	E	N	T		I	H	O	P	
	O	T	T			P	A	S	T	O	R	A	L	
B	E	F	O	G		S	O	R	E		H	O	B	O
I	T	O		O	P	H	E	L	I	A		O	E	R
L	O	O	N		A	U	T	O		M	U	F	T	I
	E	N	T	R	U	S	T	S		R	A	T		
		S	A	N	E			R	E	S	O	R	T	
P	U	T		W	O	O	D	E	N	S	P	O	O	N
E	C	O	L	I		N	E	E	D		I	N	T	O
A	L	O	E	S		E	L	S	E		A	D	E	N
S	A	L	V	E		S	E	E	R		N	O	S	E

63

S	A	T	U	P		A	S	P		R	E	N	T	A
A	C	U	T	E		V	I	A		A	R	E	A	S
T	H	R	E	E	C	E	N	T	S	W	O	R	T	H
E	E	K		W	O	R	S	E	N		D	O	S	E
			K	E	N			N	O	N	E			
	T	H	I	E	V	E	S			A	D	O	R	E
F	A	Y	E		E	R	N	E	S	T		T	E	A
E	L	E	V	E	N	G	A	L	L	O	N	H	A	T
T	O	N		S	T	O	R	M	Y		E	E	L	S
E	N	A	C	T		L	O	N	G	A	R	M		
			H	E	A	D			E	A	R			
O	L	E	O		W	I	S	E	S	T		A	L	E
S	I	X	O	C	L	O	C	K	S	H	A	D	O	W
H	E	I	S	T		D	U	E		E	R	O	S	E
A	S	T	E	R		E	D	S		R	I	S	E	S

64

A	B	D	U	L		D	E	B	U	T		A	F	T
M	A	O	R	I		E	L	I	T	E		Q	U	A
C	H	I	C	K	E	N	S	O	U	P		U	R	L
			H	E	D	Y			R	E	C	A	L	L
A	S	S	I	S	I		M	I	N	E	R			
N	E	O	N		S	W	A	N	S		U	S	S	R
E	L	M		J	O	E	Y	S		M	E	H	T	A
M	E	A	T	A	N	D	P	O	T	A	T	O	E	S
I	N	L	A	W		D	O	L	O	R		G	E	T
C	A	I	N		C	E	L	E	B		M	U	L	E
			G	L	A	D	E		A	T	O	N	E	R
B	U	N	Y	A	N			E	G	I	S			
E	N	E		P	I	E	C	E	O	F	C	A	K	E
L	I	V		A	N	N	U	L		F	O	R	E	S
A	X	E		Z	E	S	T	S		S	W	I	G	S

65

```
O P T S   S C R A P   M E S A
L O O T   C H I L E   I L E X
A O N E   R A N T O   N A M E
F L I P P I N G O N E S L I D
      P A M       Y E T
M A N E T   A C T   K R U P A
E R E   T E L L E R   E T A S
Z I P P I N G O N E S L I P S
Z E A L   D E N O T E   L E A
O L L I E   R E N   L E E R Y
      M L I       S E X
T I P P I N G O N E S H A N D
E D I T   A I D E D   A C E D
A L S O   L L A M A   L I R A
M E A N   L A Y O N   E D D Y
```

66

```
L I M N   T R A P   A F E W
A R O O   R A M O S   L U L U
B E R T   A N E R A   I L E S
A F I S H   I S O S C E L E S
N U T O I L   S U S A N S
  L A S S O S   S E T   T H E
    U S U R P   S O S O O N
M A W R   S O S   A P E D
S P I E L S   E P S O M
S U N   Y E P   Y E S M A N
    D O R I E S   E L Y S E E
E S P R E S S O S   O S T E R
G L I B   M E S A S   O R D O
G A P E   S T A G E   S A L S
O P E D   A D E N   A L E E
```

67

```
M A S S   C A S A   S L O B
E A T A   P A P A L   T O G A
S A U L   I N A L L   A U R A
H A V E O V E R A B A R R E L
    M H O       D U B
A P E   S T E M   T U R E E N
S E L F   A L E S   T A B L E
C A L L A L L T H E S H O T S
O C E A N   E R I N   S L O T
T E N N I S   O N A N   A N S
    M A E       M B A
H O L D A L L T H E C A R D S
A R E A   A F O O L   H A I L
S C A R   M I L L S   E T N A
P S S T   I N D Y   D E E M
```

68

```
A S P E R   E S T E   F R Y E
C H A F E   C H A R   L E A S
O U T T A   R A R E C O I N S
W E S   C H U M P C H A N G E
    Y E T I   S T A T
S E C T   N E E   T E P I D
E L L A   D A T A   T R I P E
A L I   F I S H F R Y   G A L
T E N S E   T O R E   P E S T
S N E E R   S O L   R O S S
    E R A S   I R O N
S U C K E R P U N C H   P E G
U P P E R C A S E   O P E R A
I T O R   E D D A   D I A L M
T O S S   D E A R   A P S E S
```

69

```
A C T   H A L T S   A M B E R
C I A   A B O U T   M A L T A
C A R   S U N N Y S I D E U P
T O A S T S   A X E   D A D S
    P E E T     W R O T E
C L E A R S A I L I N G
H E A R T   G R I N S   M O B
O G R E   G R I E G   N E M O
P O P   C R A S S   S O N A R
    B R I G H T F U T U R E
  S T R O P     O R B S
S H O E   P S A   A V O U C H
W A R M W E L C O M E   M O O
A L T E R   O L D E R   P A L
T E E N Y   G U E S T   S L Y
```

70

```
C A T E R   M A D A M   R C A
B L A S E   O X I D E   Y A M
S I M P L E S I M O N   A N I
      A P E S     T U N E S
S E R A P E S   L I O N E S S
H E A R S E   M A T R I X
E R N I E   C E D E S   P A M
A I D A   S A L E M   T R E E
F E Y   A A R O N   D O E R S
    S A I G O N   P E R S I A
A N A G R A M   B R A I S E S
S A V E S   S L E D
I D A   H E Y H E Y P A U L A
D I G   I N D U S   A S K E D
E R E   P O S T S   N E E D S
```

71

P	A	T	C	H		E	L	S	E			T	I	F	F
A	L	O	H	A		N	E	T	S			H	O	U	R
R	E	L	I	C		L	Y	E	S			A	N	N	O
R	E	D	S	K	Y	A	T	M	O	R	N	I	N	G	
		E	E	R	I	E			O	K	A	Y	S		
F	I	E	L	D	S			R	E	V	S				
A	C	R	E			P	O	I	S	E		I	V	E	
D	O	G	D	A	Y	A	F	T	E	R	N	O	O	N	
E	N	S		S	E	N	T	A			A	N	T	I	
			P	S	S	T			A	M	U	S	E	D	
A	D	O	R	E		O	R	N	O	T					
M	R	S	A	T	U	R	D	A	Y	N	I	G	H	T	
A	E	O	N		S	A	I	D		I	C	I	E	R	
T	A	L	K		E	T	U	I		E	A	G	L	E	
I	D	E	S		D	E	M	I		S	L	I	M	E	

72

P	E	R	E		C	H	E	F		P	E	W	E	E
A	L	A	S		H	E	R	O		O	P	A	L	S
V	A	N	S		A	N	N	E		P	I	L	L	S
L	I	C	O	R	I	C	E	S	T	I	C	K		
O	N	O		O	N	E			I	N	S	O	L	E
V	E	R	S	U	S		V	A	L			V	I	A
			E	N	A	T	I	C		S	L	E	E	T
S	A	N	D	W	I	C	H	B	O	A	R	D		
P	O	N	D	S		M	A	Y	A	N	S			
A	F	T		H	E	R			S	A	T	I	R	E
T	A	I	P	E	I		G	E	T		B	O	X	
P	A	N	C	A	K	E	M	A	K	E	U	P		
A	B	O	U	T		M	I	N	E		O	R	S	O
P	U	L	S	E		I	C	O	N		B	I	T	S
E	M	E	E	R		S	K	A	T		E	A	S	E

73

T	I	L	E	S		S	T	I	R		W	O	M	B
A	C	O	R	N		T	O	N	E		A	R	E	A
J	U	L	I	A		A	R	C	S		I	N	C	L
		K	I	L	L	T	H	E	C	L	O	C	K	
L	E	T		L	I	K	E		A	R	E	N	A	S
E	L	A	P	S	E			M	R	E	D			
A	I	R	S		R	E	A	C	T		M	I	A	
S	T	R	I	K	E	U	P	T	H	E	B	A	N	D
H	E	Y		A	L	I	A	S		I	N	F	O	
			B	R	A	N			E	D	G	I	E	R
A	C	R	O	S	S		R	I	M	E		A	R	E
S	H	O	O	T	T	H	E	C	U	R	L			
P	O	S	T		I	A	G	O		I	O	T	A	S
E	R	I	E		C	L	A	N		D	R	A	C	O
N	E	E	D		S	O	N	S		E	D	I	T	S

74

T	A	R	S		L	O	B	O		A	C	O	R	N
A	L	A	R		O	M	O	O		T	A	B	O	O
M	A	G	I	C	C	A	R	P	E	T	R	I	D	E
S	S	S		O	K	R	A		W	E	A	S	E	L
			S	O	B	S		T	E	N	T			
N	I	K	K	O		B	I	R	D	S	O	N	G	
P	O	N	Y	E	X	P	R	E	S	S		M	O	A
L	O	S	E		L	E	I				F	A	N	G
O	N	E		C	L	O	W	N	P	R	I	N	C	E
W	E	T	S	U	I	T	S		A	E	R	I	E	
			O	R	T	S		S	P	A	M			
E	L	F	I	S	H		E	T	A	L		S	E	T
B	A	L	L	O	O	N	P	A	Y	M	E	N	T	S
E	M	E	E	R		B	E	T	A		T	I	N	A
N	E	E	D	Y		C	E	E	S		S	T	A	R

75

A	A	H	S		E	W	E	R		S	A	L	O	N
S	W	A	T		N	O	A	H		P	L	A	N	E
P	A	V	E		C	O	R	E		H	A	S	T	A
I	R	E		C	A	L	L	T	H	E	S	H	O	T
C	E	N	S	U	S		S	T	A	R	K			
		O	G	R	E	S			S	E	A	B	E	D
L	O	F	T	S		O	P	E	N		N	U	D	E
A	P	E		E	F	F	O	R	T	S		Y	I	N
B	E	A	D		L	A	I	R		P	A	T	T	Y
S	C	R	I	B	E			S	M	I	T	H		
			V	I	S	T	A		A	L	T	E	R	S
T	A	K	E	T	H	E	F	A	L	L		F	E	E
O	V	E	R	T		L	O	O	T		P	A	C	E
R	I	N	S	E		L	O	N	E		T	R	A	M
A	S	T	E	R		S	L	E	D		A	M	P	S

76

S	O	T		F	A	B	L	E		W	H	A	L	E
O	N	E		I	D	E	A	S		R	O	L	E	X
F	A	N	T	A	S	T	I	C	V	O	Y	A	G	E
T	I	E	R	S		C	A	E	N		B	A	R	
A	R	T	I	C	L	E		P	I	G		A	L	T
			G	O	O	D	F	E	L	L	A	S		
R	A	M		A	G	E			Y	E	T	I	S	
A	L	A	S		D	E	M	O	S		C	E	D	E
H	A	R	P	O		U	K	E		R	O	E		
		M	Y	F	A	I	R	L	A	D	Y			
L	E	O		F	U	R		A	R	O	U	S	E	R
E	T	S		C	L	E	F		U	L	T	R	A	
T	H	E	B	A	D	N	E	W	S	B	E	A	R	S
G	A	T	E	S		E	M	A	I	L		F	O	P
O	N	S	E	T		S	A	N	D	Y		F	L	Y

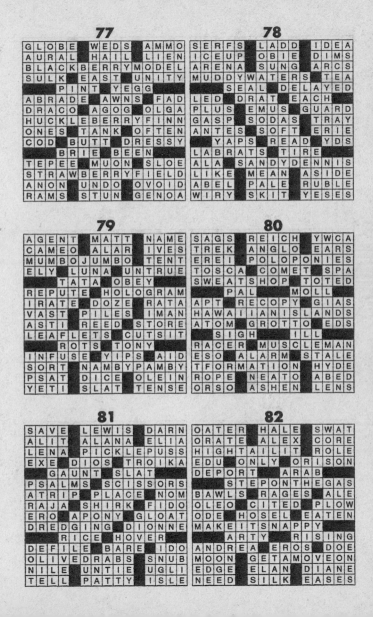

77

GLOBE · WEDS · AMMO
AURAL · HAIL · LIEN
BLACKBERRYMODEL
SULK · EAST · UNITY
· PINT · YEGG
ABRADE · AWNS · FAD
DRACO · AGOG · OLGA
HUCKLEBERRYFINN
ONES · TANK · OFTEN
COD · BUTT · DRESSY
· BRIE · BEEN
TEPEE · MUON · SLOE
STRAWBERRYFIELD
ANON · UNDO · OVOID
RAMS · STUN · GENOA

78

SERFS · LADD · IDEA
ICEUP · OBIE · DIMS
ARENA · SUNG · ARCS
MUDDYWATERS · TEA
· SEAL · DELAYED
LED · DRAT · EACH
PLUS · EMUS · GUARD
GASP · SODAS · TRAY
ANTES · SOFT · ERIE
· YAPS · READ · YDS
LABRATS · TIRE
ALA · SANDYDENNIS
LIKE · MEAN · ASIDE
ABEL · PALE · RUBLE
WIRY · SKIT · YESES

79

AGENT · MATT · NAME
CAMEO · ALAR · IVES
MUMBOJUMBO · TENT
ELY · LUNA · UNTRUE
· TATA · OBEY
REPUTE · HOLOGRAM
IRATE · DOZE · RATA
VAST · PILES · IMAN
ASTI · REED · STORE
LEAFLETS · CUTSIT
· ROTS · TONY
INFUSE · YIPS · AID
SORT · NAMBYPAMBY
PSAT · DICE · OLEIN
YETI · SLAT · TENSE

80

SAGS · REICH · YWCA
TREK · ANGLO · EARS
EREI · POLOPONIES
TOSCA · COMET · SPA
SWEATSHOP · TOTED
· PAL · MOLL
APT · RECOPY · GIAS
HAWAIIANISLANDS
ATOM · GROTTO · EDS
· SIGH · ILL
RACER · MUSCLEMAN
ESO · ALARM · STALE
TFORMATION · HYDE
ROPE · NEATO · ABED
ORSO · ASHEN · LENS

81

SAVE · LEWIS · DARN
ALIT · ALANA · ELIA
LENA · PICKLEPUSS
EXE · DIOS · TROIKA
· GAUNT · SLAT
PSALMS · SCISSORS
ATRIP · PLACE · NOM
RAJA · SHIRK · FIDO
ERO · APONY · GLOAT
DREDGING · DIONNE
· RICE · HOVER
DEFILE · BARE · IDO
OLIVEDRABS · SNUB
NILE · UNTIE · UGLI
TELL · PATTY · ISLE

82

OATER · HALE · SWAT
ORATE · ALEX · CORE
HIGHTAILIT · ROLE
EDU · ONLY · ORISON
DEPORT · ARAB
STEPONTHEGAS
BAWLS · RAGES · ALE
OLEO · CITED · PLOW
ODE · HOSEL · EATEN
MAKEITSNAPPY
· ARTY · RISING
ANDREA · EROS · DOE
MOON · GETAMOVEON
EDGE · ELAN · DIANE
NEED · SILK · EASES

83

```
A R N A Z   F U M E   F E T A
Y O U R E   I N O R   I V A N
E N T E R P R I S E A G E N T
S S S   O U S T S   M A R G E
      L I N T   F O R
A S P E N S   T A L K O V E R
I M A G O   T A I F   E L I
M A S O N T H R O W W O R L D
A S S   R I O T   A G G I E
T H E S A I N T   D U R E S S
      A B O   P O K E
S H A D E   M E L E E   M A P
H A N D L O A D E R S T Y L E
A L E E   A R I A   H A S T O
G O W N   F E E T   A X T O N
```

84

```
M B A S   G R A T A   O K R A
A L E C   R E B E L   V E A L
T A R O   A P O R T   E Y R E
H O L D Y O U R H O R S E S
      D U H   Y E N S
E O S   B A B A   A S I D E
A N T I   I A N S   E G R E T
S T A N D R I G H T H E R E
T O R T E   T R E E   T A I L
P E E P S   Y A M S   M E L
      R O P E   P I E
S T O P T H E P R E S S E S
L I A R   E L L A S   S A K E
A N T E   R E A C T   A V E R
P E S T   E R N E S   Y E W S
```

85

```
S O S A D   C Z A R   R S V P
A A N D E   R O P E   A L E E
G R A S S R O O T S   N I N E
A S P   P O P S   T A K E U P
      M O W S   B E W A R E S
A D M I T S   L E A N N
L O A D S   S E A S   D R I P
A V I D   S H A D Y   F A C E
S E L L   C U P S   B I Z E T
      E A R N S   V A L E T S
A P A C H E S   W I S E
T A X L A W   C I T E   L E S
H U L A   C O M M O N F O L K
O L E S   A T O P   J U L I E
S A S S   P O N Y   I N L A W
```

86

```
S P C A   D E P T H   A W L S
A L A S   E R O S E   C O O L
S I L K S C R E E N   T O N E
H E I F E R S   N A I L E D
      O N E   A N A L O G
M A C R A E   L A S T N A M E
I P O   T R E A T   S T A R
D O T   E S S   A R S   H U G
A R T S   T O L E T   E D O
S T O P O V E R   F E R R E T
      N E V E R S   E V A
H A B E A S   E R E C T E D
A X E D   S U E D E S H O E S
V O L E   E L L I E   E R G O
E N T R   L E F T S   L E S S
```

87

```
S A K I   S H U S H   P A S T
O P E N   P A R T I   A C H E
U S E D C A R S A L E S M A N
R E P E L   M A R L A   E M T
      E A U       E R R
O L D S C H O O L T I E S
F R O   P L A Z A   H O M E S
O D O R   A M O R E   T O N E
R E S I N   E N E M Y   T O E
    R E C Y C L E D P A P E R
      A L A       S T U
T W A   O R T H O   E M B E R
S E C O N D H A N D S M O K E
A V E R   E R I C A   E D E N
R E S T   R U L E R   L E S T
```

88

```
B O S C   R A B I D     F E E
A B A R   E V A D E S   L A X
A I R A P P A R E N T   O T C
S T A I R     D A T A   U N O
      G I S H   L A T E R O N
J A B   N E A P   L U M P
A B O U T A D A M   S C O R E
D I A S   S I N A I   E W E R
E G R E T   T E N S P E E D S
      D U E S   S I L O   R O E
E L S P E T H   C E L T
N U T   O R E O   A R A B S
D C I   F A L S E P R O F I T
O A F   F I L L E R   M A K E
N S F   N O O N E   P R E P
```

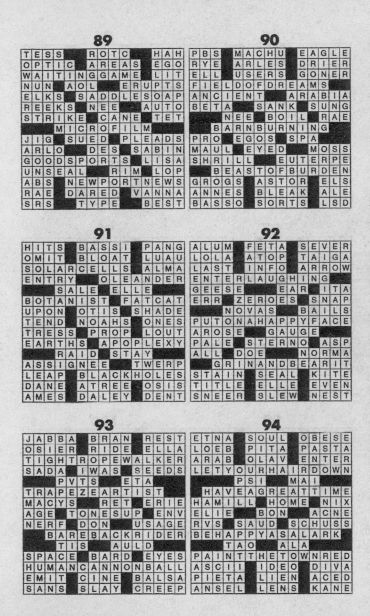

89

T	E	S	S		R	O	T	C		H	A	H
O	P	T	I	C		A	R	E	A	S		E	G	O
W	A	I	T	I	N	G	G	A	M	E		L	I	T
N	U	N		A	O	L		E	R	U	P	T	S
E	L	K	S		S	A	D	D	L	E	S	O	A	P
R	E	E	K	S		N	E	E		A	U	T	O
S	T	R	I	K	E		C	A	N	E		T	E	T
	M	I	C	R	O	F	I	L	M
J	I	G		S	U	E	D		P	L	E	A	D	S
A	R	L	O		D	E	S		S	A	B	I	N
G	O	O	D	S	P	O	R	T	S		L	I	S	A
U	N	S	E	A	L		R	I	M		L	O	P
A	B	S		N	E	W	P	O	R	T	N	E	W	S
R	A	E		D	A	R	E	D		V	A	N	N	A
S	R	S		T	Y	P	E		B	E	S	T

90

P	B	S		M	A	C	H	U		E	A	G	L	E
R	Y	E		A	R	L	E	S		D	R	I	E	R
E	L	L		U	S	E	R	S		G	O	N	E	R
F	I	E	L	D	O	F	D	R	E	A	M	S
A	N	C	I	E	N	T		A	R	A	B	I	A
B	E	T	A		S	A	N	K		S	U	N	G
	N	E	E		B	O	I	L		R	A	E
	B	A	R	N	B	U	R	N	I	N	G
P	R	O		E	G	O	S		S	P	A
M	A	U	L		E	Y	E	D		M	O	S	S
S	H	R	I	L	L		E	U	T	E	R	P	E
B	E	A	S	T	O	F	B	U	R	D	E	N
G	R	O	G	S		A	S	T	O	R		E	L	S
A	N	N	E	S		B	L	E	A	K		A	L	E
B	A	S	S	O		S	O	R	T	S		L	S	D

91

H	I	T	S		B	A	S	S	I		P	A	N	G
O	M	I	T		B	L	O	A	T		L	U	A	U
S	O	L	A	R	C	E	L	L	S		A	L	M	A
E	N	T	R	Y		O	L	E	A	N	D	E	R
	S	A	L	E		E	L	L	E
B	O	T	A	N	I	S	T		F	A	T	C	A	T
U	P	O	N		O	T	I	S		S	H	A	D	E
T	E	N	D		N	O	A	H	S		O	N	E	S
T	R	E	S	S		P	R	O	P		L	O	U	T
E	A	R	T	H	S		A	P	O	P	L	E	X	Y
	R	A	I	D		S	T	A	Y
A	S	S	I	G	N	E	E		T	W	E	R	P
L	E	A	P		B	L	A	C	K	H	O	L	E	S
D	A	N	E		A	T	R	E	E		O	S	I	S
A	M	E	S		D	A	L	E	Y		D	E	N	T

92

A	L	U	M		F	E	T	A		S	E	V	E	R
L	O	L	A		A	T	O	P		T	A	I	G	A
L	A	S	T		I	N	F	O		A	R	R	O	W
E	N	T	E	R	L	A	U	G	H	I	N	G
G	E	E	S	E		E	A	R		I	T	A
E	R	R		Z	E	R	O	E	S		S	N	A	P
	N	O	V	A	S		B	A	I	L	S
P	U	T	O	N	A	H	A	P	P	Y	F	A	C	E
A	R	O	S	E		G	A	U	G	E
P	A	L	E		S	T	E	R	N	O		A	S	P
A	L	L		D	O	E		N	O	R	M	A
G	R	I	N	A	N	D	B	E	A	R	I	T
S	T	A	I	N		S	E	A	L		K	I	T	E
T	I	T	L	E		E	L	L	E		E	V	E	N
S	N	E	E	R		S	L	E	W		N	E	S	T

93

J	A	B	B	A		B	R	A	N		R	E	S	T
O	S	I	E	R		R	I	D	E		E	L	L	A
T	I	G	H	T	R	O	P	E	W	A	L	K	E	R
S	A	D	A		I	W	A	S		S	E	E	D	S
	P	V	T	S		E	T	A
T	R	A	P	E	Z	E	A	R	T	I	S	T
M	A	C	Y	S		R	E	T		E	R	I	E
A	G	E		T	O	N	E	S	U	P		E	N	V
N	E	R	F		D	O	N		U	S	A	G	E
	B	A	R	E	B	A	C	K	R	I	D	E	R
	T	I	S		A	U	L	D
S	P	A	C	E		B	A	R	D		E	Y	E	S
H	U	M	A	N	C	A	N	N	O	N	B	A	L	L
E	M	I	T		C	I	N	E		B	A	L	S	A
S	A	N	S		S	L	A	Y		C	R	E	E	P

94

E	T	N	A		S	O	U	L		O	B	E	S	E
L	O	E	B		P	I	T	A		P	A	S	T	A
A	R	A	B		O	L	A	V		E	N	T	E	R
L	E	T	Y	O	U	R	H	A	I	R	D	O	W	N
	P	S	I		M	A	I
H	A	V	E	A	G	R	E	A	T	T	I	M	E
H	A	M	I	L	L		H	O	M	E		N	I	X
E	L	I	E		B	O	N		A	C	N	E
R	V	S		S	A	U	D		S	C	H	U	S	S
B	E	H	A	P	P	Y	A	S	A	L	A	R	K
	T	A	O		A	L	A
P	A	I	N	T	T	H	E	T	O	W	N	R	E	D
A	S	C	I	I		I	D	E	O		D	I	V	A
P	I	E	T	A		L	I	E	N		A	C	E	D
A	N	S	E	L		L	E	N	S		K	A	N	E

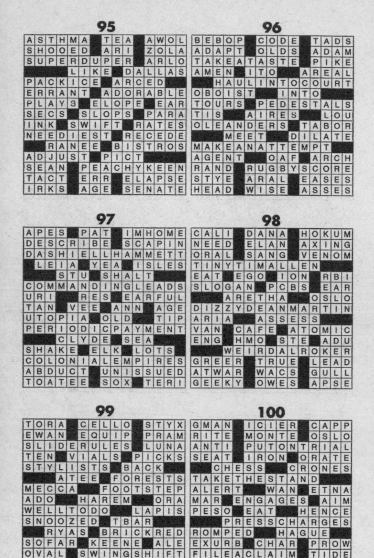

95

A	S	T	H	M	A		T	E	A		A	W	O	L
S	H	O	O	E	D		A	R	I		Z	O	L	A
S	U	P	E	R	D	U	P	E	R		A	R	L	O
		L	I	K	E		D	A	L	L	A	S		
P	A	C	K	I	C	E		A	R	C	E	D		
E	R	R	A	N	T		A	D	O	R	A	B	L	E
P	L	A	Y	3		E	L	O	P	E		E	A	R
S	E	C	S		S	L	O	P	S		P	A	R	A
I	N	K		S	W	I	F	T		R	A	T	E	S
N	E	E	D	I	E	S	T		R	E	C	E	D	E
		R	A	N	E	E		B	I	S	T	R	O	S
		A	D	J	U	S	T		P	I	C	T		
S	E	A	N		P	E	A	C	H	Y	K	E	E	N
T	A	C	T		E	R	R		E	L	A	P	S	E
I	R	K	S		A	G	E		S	E	N	A	T	E

96

B	E	B	O	P		C	O	D	E		T	A	D	S
A	D	A	P	T		O	L	D	S		A	D	A	M
T	A	K	E	A	T	A	S	T	E		P	I	K	E
A	M	E	N		I	T	O		A	R	E	A	L	
			H	A	U	L	I	N	T	O	C	O	U	R	T
O	B	O	I	S	T			I	N	T	O			
T	O	U	R	S		P	E	D	E	S	T	A	L	S
T	I	S		A	I	R	E	S				L	O	U
O	L	E	A	N	D	E	R	S		T	A	B	O	R
			M	E	E	T			D	I	L	A	T	E
M	A	K	E	A	N	A	T	T	E	M	P	T		
A	G	E	N	T			O	A	F		A	R	C	H
R	A	N	D		R	U	G	B	Y	S	C	O	R	E
S	T	Y	E		A	R	A	L		E	A	S	E	S
H	E	A	D		W	I	S	E		A	S	S	E	S

97

A	P	E	S		P	A	T		I	M	H	O	M	E
D	E	S	C	R	I	B	E		S	C	A	P	I	N
D	A	S	H	I	E	L	L	H	A	M	M	E	T	T
		L	E	I	A		Y	E	A		I	S	L	E	S
			S	T	U		S	H	A	L	T			
C	O	M	M	A	N	D	I	N	G	L	E	A	D	S
U	R	I		R	E	S		E	A	R	F	U	L	
T	A	N		V	E	E		A	N	N		A	G	E
U	T	O	P	I	A		O	L	D		T	I	P	
P	E	R	I	O	D	I	C	P	A	Y	M	E	N	T
			C	L	Y	D	E		S	E	A			
S	H	A	K	E		E	L	K		L	O	T	S	
C	O	L	O	N	I	A	L	E	M	P	I	R	E	S
A	B	D	U	C	T		U	N	I	S	S	U	E	D
T	O	A	T	E	E		S	O	X		T	E	R	I

98

C	A	L	I		D	A	N	A		H	O	K	U	M
N	E	E	D		E	L	A	N		A	X	I	N	G
O	R	A	L		S	A	N	G		V	E	N	O	M
T	I	N	Y	T	I	M	A	L	L	E	N			
E	A	T		E	G	O		I	O	N		R	B	I
S	L	O	G	A	N		P	C	B	S		E	A	R
			A	R	E	T	H	A			O	S	L	O
D	I	Z	Z	Y	D	E	A	N	M	A	R	T	I	N
A	R	I	A			A	S	S	E	S	S			
V	A	N		C	A	F	E		A	T	O	M	I	C
E	N	G		H	M	O		S	T	E		A	D	U
			W	E	I	R	D	A	L	R	O	K	E	R
G	R	E	E	R		T	R	U	E		L	E	A	D
A	T	W	A	R		W	A	C	S		G	U	L	L
G	E	E	K	Y		O	W	E	S		A	P	S	E

99

T	O	R	A		C	E	L	L	O		S	T	Y	X
E	W	A	N		E	Q	U	I	P		P	R	A	M
S	L	I	D	E	R	U	L	E	S		L	U	N	A
T	E	N		V	I	A	L	S		P	I	C	K	S
S	T	Y	L	I	S	T	S		B	A	C	K		
			A	T	E	E		F	O	R	E	S	T	S
M	E	C	C	A		F	O	O	T	S	T	E	P	
A	D	O		H	A	R	E	M		O	R	A		
W	E	L	L	L	T	O	D	O		L	A	P	I	S
S	N	O	O	Z	E	D		T	B	A	R			
		R	Y	A	S		B	R	I	C	K	R	E	D
S	O	F	A	R		K	E	E	N	E		A	L	E
O	V	A	L		S	W	I	N	G	S	H	I	F	T
F	E	S	T		D	A	N	C	E		A	S	I	A
A	R	T	Y		S	I	G	H	S		D	E	N	T

100

G	M	A	N		I	C	I	E	R		C	A	P	P
R	I	T	E		M	O	N	T	E		O	S	L	O
A	N	T	I		P	U	T	O	N	T	R	I	A	L
S	E	A	T		I	R	O	N		O	R	A	T	E
			C	H	E	S	S		C	R	O	N	E	S
T	A	K	E	T	H	E	S	T	A	N	D			
A	L	E	R	T		W	A	N		E	T	N	A	
M	A	R		E	N	G	A	G	E	S		A	I	M
P	E	S	O		E	A	T		H	E	N	C	E	
			P	R	E	S	S	C	H	A	R	G	E	S
R	O	M	P	E	D			H	A	G	U	E		
E	X	U	R	B		C	H	A	R		P	R	O	W
F	I	L	E	A	C	L	A	I	M		T	I	D	E
I	D	E	S		H	O	U	S	E		E	N	I	D
T	E	S	S		I	D	L	E	D		D	E	N	S